SUMMER CAMP

SUMMER CAMP

A MAINE CAMP DIRECTOR REMEMBERS

BY RON FURST

2018
Great Life Press
Rye, New Hampshire

ISBN: 978-1-938394-31-7
Library of Congress Control Number: 2018932964

Published by:
Great Life Press
Rye, New Hampshire 03870
www.greatlifepress.com

Book design: Grace Peirce
Paintings, front and back cover: Gordon Carlisle

Additional books are available from:
email: info@camphawthorne.org

The stories in this book are based on the author's personal experiences. Some names have been changed.

*To the many campers and staff
who generously shared their joy
and energy with my wife and
me during our twenty-four years
together at*
Camp Hawthorne

Contents

Preface

I believe that one of life's greatest privileges is to be able to support your loved ones by working in a career that you truly love. Now that I am retired from an active role in the camping industry, I have had more than adequate time to look back at how I managed to create a business that was so much fun.

Our lives are made up of stories. We all have them; some are more interesting than others, but they define our lives, and each brings us the gift of a lesson if we are able to see it. My stories have given me great gifts; indeed, the greatest has been to understand that I haven't managed alone. Once I had a clear mental picture of where I wanted to go in my life, a helpful hand was often extended at crucial moments. Help came from material and nonmaterial realms guiding me toward certain situations that proved useful to me. This intuitive help, I believe, is offered to all from the deeper recesses of our minds, if only we are open to it. Once I learned to trust my inner guidance, I knew the result of my promptings would lead me where I needed to go.

My hope is that I can be of service to others in a more advisory capacity, and that these stories of my life will bring a lightness to your heart and be an inspiration to your soul.

Introduction

Writing my book of stories began four years after Camp Hawthorne closed in 2010. My memories of camp life have grown more vivid as the years have passed. Now, mostly, I remember the fun we all had, not the hard work and long hours required of a camp director. I deeply enjoyed all twenty-four seasons on Panther Pond in Raymond, Maine. No other career choice could have been more suited to my talents and sensibilities than the role of camp director.

Many movies, TV shows, and books popularize the culture of children's overnight camps. I understand their need to entertain the public, but can't help being offended by a common theme that the camp director is some kind of buffoon, out of touch with the hidden behaviors of his campers and staff. Perhaps my memoir can give the reader an accurate understanding of what is involved in running a camp.

My job was similar to being the mayor of a small city. I was responsible for the physical, emotional, and spiritual well-being of my community twenty-four hours a day. When the phone rang at camp—and it did throughout the day and early evening—it was usually for me. I carried a portable phone so I could answer each call. Our office manager answered the phone only when I was away from camp or running an activity like driving the motorboat or officiating a track meet. Parents seemed thankful to find me on the other end of the phone.

Within a few minutes of any day my role could switch from being camp cheerleader to healer of homesickness, back-up cook, storyteller, minister, bank teller, bookkeeper, orthodontist (I learned to fix braces with needlenose pliers), travel agent, jokester, and master plumber—to name just a few.

Campers and staff constantly needed my attention, approval, support, ideas, and cash. I carried a sizable wad of money in my pocket to cover the endless trips to the hardware store, crafts supply store, ice cream parlor (named the mosquito) and local supermarket, since we were always running out of something at the last minute. Everyone constantly needed my attention for something, and it was my pleasure to help.

I loved my job and felt responsible for everyone's well-being. If a thunder storm started to rumble in the middle of the night, I knew I needed to be in the center of camp, flashlight in hand and ready to calm the nerves of my community. If a camper was sick in the middle of the night, and needed to be transported to the hospital immediately, that was often my job as well.

Of all my responsibilities at camp I most enjoyed taking campers for rides on a large tube behind our motorboat. We had a two-person tube so campers could share the experience with a friend. Many campers wanted a fast ride that would take the tube over the wake from the boat and bounce them around a bit. I would accommodate them, always being careful not to overdo it. I knew my customers and gave a moderate ride to those who needed a less thrilling tubing experience.

Around 4:00 each afternoon I would lead a camp meeting, right after our break for milk and cookies. The meeting was to inform campers what activities were being offered for their optional period. Choices might include sailing, archery, swimming, kayaking, canoeing, crafts, and always tubing.

To help create camper enthusiasm for tubing, I would make up a new name for the thrilling rides I was offering that period. I enjoyed coming up with funny names, like "The Circle of Death," "Suicide 6," "The Devils Doughnut," "One Day in Hell," "The Squasher," and "Momma, I Lost My Shorts." In reality, all the rides were exactly the same, but the campers were certain they were all different. They would squeal with delight as I ferried them around the lake.

The following stories are some of my most vivid and favorite memories of my career as camp director of Camp Hawthorne. I hope you enjoy them.

Summer Camp in the 1950s

Summer Camp in the 1950s

My personal exploration into the meaning of life began during my early elementary school years. I remember lying on the grass, staring up at the clouds moving across the sky and asking myself, "What is life? What is life?" On occasion, after several minutes of repeating this mantra, my awareness would flip for a moment into a subtle and unexplainable sense of spiritual reverie. This feeling became more meaningful when I began having a series of numinous dreams involving magical landscapes with deeply loving animals and people.

These experiences occurred most frequently during my first few years at camp in Maine, around age eight. I kept quiet about my early spiritual awareness. I thought it too hard to explain to my family or young friends.

My first summer at sleep away camp was 1953. I had

just turned six years old a few days before leaving home for eight weeks of camp, virtually the whole summer.

What I remember most about those years at camp was living in a beautiful natural setting surrounded by caring and fun-loving young adults. The camp was situated on Coffee Pond in Casco, Maine, nestled in a forest of white pine trees. Camps back then were heavily forested, with few athletic fields. The strong smell of pine was everywhere. How could anyone be unhappy living in a place that smelled so good?

The quality of light caused by the angle of the sun as it reflected off the still water of the lake, added a sense of magic to camp. Walking under the stars along the lakeshore after an evening of storytelling by the campfire, was nothing I could have experienced at home. I loved spending the summers at camp and could not wait to return each year. It's no wonder I chose a career in camping.

As a young camper, I was on the lookout to form relationships with camp counselors and directors who seemed open to getting to know me. Young boys are often looking for male role models. My childhood camp had no shortage of interesting possibilities. I was fortunate to find many adults who could understand a sensitive child like me. When I think today about the adults I wanted to emulate, I believe I was choosing wisely.

I formed a strong bond with a counselor named Arthur. He was not my bunk counselor, but was stationed a few cabins down the row with campers older than I. He was probably a junior or senior in college at the time we first met. Arthur was one of the few counselors who were not hired to coach or teach an athletic sport. He ran the arts and crafts program and was always assigned to the crafts cabin that was built by the lake on the far end of camp by the soccer field.

Whenever there was an open period where I could choose an activity, my choice was always to be with Arthur at crafts. My bunkmates most often headed for the waterfront for free swim. Arthur was extremely patient and always available to help me start a project, from learning how to make a key chain out of gimp, or a hand built clay ashtray fired in the camp kiln, where it would almost always explode into a thousand pieces.

At the end of the period I would be the last to leave the crafts building so I could walk back to my cabin with him, chatting all the way. He was interested in hearing what I had to say about my experiences at camp. Arthur was a thoughtful person who might not have gelled that well with the sports-minded staff. At the time I did not know that he was preparing to go to medical school.

Sunday dinner was always a cookout; each cabin would cook dinner over a pine fire in a rustic fire pit by their cabin. Our counselors rushed us through dinner so they could head to the field for the weekly counselor softball game. The teams were always the new staff against the returning staff. This was not a casual game. It was a grudge match for bragging rights where a spontaneous fistfight was always a possibility. I have to admit I loved this camp tradition and could not wait to play in the Sunday softball game, when I later became a counselor.

A weekly campfire followed the game. The campfire site was perched on a hill that overlooked the field. Two of our camp directors, both named Henry, were talented storytellers. We all looked forward to their stories. It was Arthur's job to build a wood structure each week that related to the story we were about to hear that evening and that would burn in the fire.

While most of the camp was watching the game, I would volunteer to help Arthur set up for the campfire. I remember a story about a racecar driver that required a structure that looked like a racecar. My job was always to fill the inside of the structure with twigs and pine needles to assure that the wood would easily catch on fire and burn evenly.

One Sunday evening we finished early preparing for the evening's campfire and sat on the hill together overlooking the ball game. I don't remember how we got on the subject, but Arthur started to talk about how surprised he was that my older brother and I were so different in our interests and personalities. My brother was three years older and was well liked at camp. However, Arthur could see that we just approached our young lives differently. I was spellbound when he shared his observations. I felt his understanding and support of me on a very deep level. I was grateful that he took the time to understand me and often think back to our talk on the hill that early evening. It could only have happened at camp.

Camp offered me a variety of wonderful young men I would emulate in my life. Arthur was the first, followed by other, more sports-minded adults, as I grew older. My most sustaining role models were our camp directors. It was because of them that I chose a career in camping. I know many boys would say that their role model was their father or grandfather; or maybe a historical figure like Teddy Roosevelt or sports figure like Michael Jordan. For me, it was the adults I met at camp as a child who presented the blueprint of who I might become.

Camp Softball

୬

Many overnight camps back in the early 1950s were organized around competitive sports. Young campers were encouraged to try out for sports teams within their age group and, within a week of practices and skills development, sent over to a neighboring camp for a day of competition. Winning was highly prized and occasioned broad smiles from the camp directors and camp community. Losing, on the other hand, was disheartening, and a pattern of losing created feelings of inadequacy and self-loathing among the campers.

At age ten, I was determined to be part of a softball team for eleven-year-olds and younger at camp. I had never played Little League and had no established softball skills. However, I had made a good connection with Dick, the counselor who coached the team, and positioned myself to be around him whenever I could.

I finally got to be on the team as an alternate player. As a nonstarting player, I spent most of each game on the bench, which pleased me just fine; I was terrified of having someone hit a ball to me in a game that really mattered.

Our camp was only a few years old and tended to attract more young misfits than did the other camps that were in our competitive league. Our campers were more interested in sitting on our beds reading *Mad* magazine than playing serious sports. Most of us hiked up our pants much too high to look like serious athletes. Few of us saw sports as a possible career or a way out of the inner city. We had been sent to camp mostly to free our parents during the summer to go to their local country clubs. We, in turn, just wanted a carefree summer with our bunkmates until we were older and had to get serious about college.

I clearly remember my introduction to competitive sports games. Dick piled our ragtag team into the back of the camp pickup truck, our only mode of transportation to the games, and off we sped to good old Camp Mendota, a few miles down the road. Try not to be too alarmed that we were not carefully seat-belted into place. The back of the truck smelled like sour milk, since its real purpose was to make daily runs to the local dump with each day's kitchen garbage. I have to admit, being huddled together in the open air like lambs to the slaughter was fun.

Camp Mendota was neither fancy nor exclusive.

The ball field might have been a hay field just a few years earlier. Only the immediate playing area had been mowed, with high grass taking over the rest of the open space. We were led down to the field by our coach and into a rotting baseball dugout that smelled like horses had peed in it a few minutes before we arrived.

When we unloaded from the truck, our opposing team was already out on the field, warming up with batting practice and fielding drills. I wondered how they could possibly be our opponents. This was supposed to be a game for eleven-year-old players and younger. These boys were giants compared to us. Their first baseman, named Andy Finke, looked like a stand-in for Prince Fielder (currently of the Texas Rangers). Andy was strong, tall, hairy, and highly intimidating. Their other star player, we soon learned, was nicknamed "The Machine." He also looked to be fifteen or older and could cover his shortstop position like a cat. We could easily see that nothing we were capable of hitting would ever get by him. We complained to our coach that the Camp Mendota team was a bunch of cheats. As a team, we had little talent for athletics, but were highly experienced complainers.

I think our coach shared our suspicions that a serious ethics violation was happening here, but, as he said on that day, "we're here to play ball."

Both Andy Finke and The Machine batted in the middle of the batting order. Their coach, after looking us over, correctly believed that our pitcher would walk the first three batters he faced, and then Andy or The Machine would easily belt a home run for a quick four-run lead.

After about three innings, we were behind something like 26–0. Dick tried to negotiate a double header so we could start a new game that might give our players a little hope and dignity. We were not so lucky. Their true goal was to pound our little egos into the dirt.

"Night Baseball Tonight!"

⇒⊪⇐

My first paying job at age thirteen was a short stint as a waiter while attending overnight camp in Maine. Camp waiters arrived thirty minutes before each meal and had to wolf down their food in order to have time to set their two tables, each with seven campers and one counselor, before the recorded bugle call blared and two hundred starving campers and staff raced in to find seats at their assigned tables.

Camp waiters enjoyed relative celebrity that allowed them freedom of access to the kitchen and occasional extra desserts. Compensation back in 1959 was twenty-five cents a meal. Not enough to save for a car, but easily enough to keep your hidden stash of candy (Fire Balls, Tootsie Rolls, Sugar Daddys, etc.) well supplied.

The privilege of becoming a waiter was reserved for the older campers. At my camp, a veteran camper nicknamed George the Rock was headwaiter. There was an obvious pecking order among the waiters, with the strongest and most aggressive first in line to receive a full tray of food to carry to their respective tables. George was by far the strongest of our lot; everyone knew he could crush your head as easily as opening a peanut shell.

Only the most charismatic counselors were able to secure the services of George the Rock, which guaranteed that their food would arrive before anyone else's in the massive room. At our camp, two counselors named Dick and Al saw it as their birthright.

Even though Dick and Al were regular camp counselors with no supervisory or administrative power, their air of confidence and superiority led everyone to believe that they—not Henry, the camp's director—actually ran the camp. Their swagger was rooted in the fact that they attended Ivy League colleges (Cornell and Brown, respectively) and were excellent athletes to boot. Dick and Al's tables were adjacent to each other at the far end of the dining hall, in front of a towering stone fireplace. On cold or rainy days, they had a camper eating at their table light a little fire to take the chill out of the air and thus enhance their eating experience.

It took real strength and stamina to maneuver a tray loaded with two servings of chicken pie, cole slaw, and chicken noodle soup from the kitchen all the way to Dick and Al's tables. George was always first in line to receive his servings of food, which were then quickly delivered, piping hot. No one ever challenged or complained about their special treatment: it was just part of our camp's social order.

My first opportunity to become a camp waiter came during Trip Week, when the two older groups of boys left for a week's excursion to Nova Scotia and Bar Harbor, Maine. My best friend Eliot and I jumped at the chance to raise our status at camp by applying for the job. We easily convinced Henry to let us share the role of headwaiter.

A little power can be dangerous in the hands of thirteen-year-old boys.

Once we were able to convince an array of camp misfits to join our waitstaff, our next executive decision was to assign someone to replace George.

I decided that Dana would be the perfect person to get a rise out of Al and Dick. Dana was a far cry from George the Rock. He was thin as a toothpick, possessed no noticeable upper body strength, and wore bottle-thick eyeglasses. Rumor had it that his near blindness was caused by being hit in the face with a golf club on his father's back swing. Dana had little interest in camp athletics and mostly enjoyed lounging on his camp cot surrounded by a more-than-adequate collection of *Mad* magazines. Yet he was spunky and eager to please and jumped at the chance to man an honored position in the waiter's food line.

I liked Dana, and had not intended to make fun of him, having the sole goal of sending Dick and Al a gentle and funny message about their entitled attitudes.

The moment Al and Dick arrived at the dining hall to discover who had replaced their super waiter, Al went bananas. Eliot and I were immediately put on notice that a serious social wrong had been committed and if Dana did not work out to their liking, we would suffer the consequences. We just giggled to cover up our fear; camp power tasted delicious, and it was way too early to back down.

Luck had it that Dana's first meal as a waiter was on a Sunday. Each Sunday afternoon, our camp chef, Vinnie, would somehow manage to produce a big and much appreciated homemade meal, which made up for the less-than-memorable meals he produced the rest of the week.

We put Dana at the head of the line and loaded his tray with two platters of roast brisket, two bowls of mashed potatoes, two bowls of peas, and two gravy boats filled with mushroom gravy.

We helped Dana lift his tray and balance it on the palm of his right hand. He used his left hand to steady the tray as he headed to the tray stand at the far end of the dining room by Al and Dick's tables. We held our collective breath as Dana wobbled his way around an array of obstacles. Halfway to his destination, I noticed he was in trouble. The steam from the mashed potatoes had fogged up his thick eyeglasses, making it impossible for him to see where he was going. As he neared Al's table, he stumbled on Al's chair and dumped the two platters of brisket, potatoes, peas, and gravy onto Al's lap. Al's short pants only partially protected him from the deluge.

The camp community, usually accustomed to wild applause whenever a waiter lost control of his tray, fell into complete silence. Everyone knew someone was going to pay a hefty price. Al, still smothered in mushroom gravy, and with Dick by his side, stormed up to us and pronounced the three most dreaded words in camp folklore: **"Night baseball tonight!!!"**

Eliot and I had no idea what Dick and Al might be planning on our behalf, but we clearly understood that it was not going to be pleasant. The whole idea of night baseball sounded pretty sinister to me. However, both of us had always enjoyed the attention paid to us by these two very popular counselors. Besides, their camp responsibilities were to take care of us, so how harsh could it be? I did share their threat with the camp director, but he just shrugged his shoulders and acted like he had no idea what I was talking about, which I believed was the case.

Around two in the morning, two counselors with hooded sweatshirts pulled tightly around their faces came to our bunk. They instructed Eliot and me to get out of bed, put on sneakers and a long-sleeved shirt, and follow them outside. They led us to the baseball field, a five-minute walk from our cabin. When we got there, we immediately realized that we were to be the evening's entertainment.

In the light of the full moon I could see forty or so camp staff filling the bleachers on the side of the field by third base. Everyone had their faces hidden by their hooded sweatshirts. There were also two lawn chairs set up next to the bleachers, in which two more people were sitting with their faces shielded. In the bright moonlight, I could see that their toenails were painted. Oh, God, I thought, even the nurses are here.

What followed might resemble a mild hazing in college fraternities, but in actuality, it was standard camp theater back in the 1950s and not in any way mean or painful. Eliot was told to use a canoe paddle as he would a softball bat and to give me a whack on my backside. He was the batter and I, essentially, was the ball. Once I got whacked, I had to trot the bases and return to home plate. Then we changed positions, and I got to whack Eliot.

This was to be a nine-inning game, and if the counselors felt we were not striking each other hard enough, a pinch hitter was in the on-deck circle, waiting to take a swing at us. The pinch hitter was a muscular counselor and softball star named Slugger Sagansky.

Eliot and I knew we were not about to hurt one another. We each struck only hard enough for a good sound effect, then faked a yelp that drew spirited applause from the fans in the bleachers. To be honest, the most humiliating part of this spectacle was trotting around the bases. The game was called after six innings when the only available wooden paddle split in two.

We accepted our ordeal like the thirteen-year-old men we thought we were and never complained to the camp director. However, Eliot and I refused to remove Dana as Dick and Al's waiter for the rest of the week. We did substantially lighten his load and instructed him to hold his tray by his waist to keep the steam a safe distance from his eyeglasses and avoid another catastrophe.

Our revenge came unexpectedly the following evening. Evidently, the camp staff had enjoyed the past evening's festivities and felt they had the right to select two other unsuspecting campers for a game of night baseball.

One of the draftees dragged out of bed was nicknamed Fish and Chips Shapiro due to his fishing obsession. Fish and Chips Shapiro would arrive at camp each summer with a tackle box of fishing gear large enough to supply the commercial fishing fleet of Gloucester, Massachusetts. He boasted that he possessed fishing lures designed to catch fish from ocean marlin to brook trout. This was somewhat ironic since our camp was situated on a small pond that rarely offered anglers anything more interesting than sunfish and yellow perch. Nonetheless, younger campers flocked to his cabin to gawk at what appeared to be the mother of all tackle boxes with a look of excitement one might have when viewing the shrunken head exhibit at the Ripley's Believe It or Not museum.

The other draftee for the night baseball game was my good friend Barnsy Kane. Barnsy, whose real name was Howard, was given his nickname from an adaptation of his father's first name, Bernard. Barnsy's father was famous for arriving at camp on visiting day chewing mercilessly on a cigar and spitting all over the floor of our cabin. Within ten minutes of arriving at camp, he would lie down on Barnsy's bunk and sleep away the rest of the afternoon, never showing up to watch his son perform at the water ski show designed to thrill the parents.

I was really upset when Barnsy was taken from our cabin that evening and led to the field with Fish and Chips Shapiro. Eliot and I had been somewhat prepared for the ordeal, but poor Barnsy was unsuspecting and I worried how he might react.

The moon was shrouded by heavy cloud cover that night, making it hard to find your way around camp. All of my cabin mates lay awake, concerned for Barnsy.

In less than ten minutes, Barnsy came crashing through the cabin's screen door. Evidently, when rounding first base in the first inning of night baseball, he had made a run for it. The counselors had underestimated Barnsy, who, though built like a football lineman, could run at lightning speed once he got his motor going. The lack of moonlight made it easy for him to head for the cover of some woods and make his way back to our cabin.

I got the idea to hide Barnsy in the back closet of our cabin, which stored sleeping bags and athletic equipment. The closet did not have a door or a light so it was easy to cover him up in a pile of sleeping bags, where he could be undetected.

The counselors' frantic search for Barnsy aroused Henry, our camp director, who was notorious for being the world's lightest sleeper. When Dick and Al appeared outside our cabin to check if Barnsy had returned to his bed, Henry intercepted them and demanded to know what was going on.

In a flash of pure genius, I told Henry that Barnsy had returned to the cabin, crying and hysterical, and said he had had it with camp, grabbed his jacket and flashlight, and stated he was going to hike through the woods until he found a highway to hitchhike home to Massachusetts.

Henry's anger was now over the top. A camp director's greatest fear is that a camper might go AWOL. How could he ever explain to Barnsy's parents—or the Maine State Police—that Barnsy took off in the middle of the night after enduring a game of night baseball?

Henry demanded that Dick and Al organize all the other camp staff that were awake and search every inch of the camp and surrounding woods to find Barnsy, telling them he did not care if it took them all night. All the while, Barnsy, who could sleep anywhere, was snuggled under the sleeping bags, biting his cheeks so as not to laugh so loudly he would be found.

Barnsy, my cabin mates, and I fell back to sleep. Around six in the morning, I woke him up so he could return to his bed. He was discovered in the bunk around seven, after Dick and Al spent a frightful evening crawling under camp buildings and whispering Barnsy's name.

This story is what I remember from my camp experiences back in 1960. By today's standards such events might reek of bullying and college hazing behavior. But for me and my camp friends, overnight camp filled us with wonderful memories. My experiences were largely positive and character building, and led me years later to a professional career running a camp.

Children's camps have changed with the times. Everyone I know in the camping business today is highly sensitive to ensuring that their camp community is supportive to the emotional needs of all their guests.

Camp Hawthorne Collection

❧

Camp Hawthorne

I was one of those fortunate people who know at an early age what career path is right for them. Around the age of twelve, I had a strong sense that someday I would have a career as a summer camp director. How I managed to turn my early career impulse into a real business is a story in itself. While I could clearly see my future in my mind's eye, I had to hold the image for years, trusting that my life might unfold as I hoped.

Looking back, it now seems as if an invisible hand guided me to situations that would be needed to run my own camping business. After completing business school, I acquired a master's degree in counseling psychology, taught special education, completed an Outward Bound survival program, and learned the essentials of light construction and caretaking—all skills that would later prove essential in operating a summer camp.

When I turned thirty-eight, I knew it was time to

make my dream a reality. Camps were rarely for sale, and in the 1980s you needed a million dollars to close a sale. Fortunately, my ongoing interest in the camping business had led me to a retired camp director who was now buying and selling camp properties. We met for dinner, and after hearing of my interest in starting a camp, he offered me the use of a camp facility he had on the market for the upcoming summer. He must have felt that he had a better chance of selling the camp property if children were present when he showed the camp to prospective buyers. He said he would rent me the camp facility, including all the boats and equipment, for the unbelievable price of $2,000 for the season.

I had enough money set aside to print a small brochure and pay the rent but little money left over for promotion or advertising. I decided to send a brochure to the middle school in my town and ask that they post it on the office bulletin board where parents might see it. I figured that since I was offering a private program, my brochure would probably find its way into the school trash can, but thought it was worth a try.

To my amazement, a week later I received an envelope with three applications and a deposit in the mail. I couldn't believe my good fortune. I would have expected a call for references before a family would send three children to a new camp. When I called the family to thank them for the applications, I found out that the mother was the school secretary. She had opened the school mail and became interested in the camp. Instead of discarding the brochure, she took it home to show her family. Now I had the confidence to move ahead and $750 to invest in advertising. Before the summer season began, I was able to sign up twenty-eight campers to start my new program.

Unfortunately, the camp I was renting was sold at the end of that summer, which required that I find a new home for the camp. I now had to face the possibility of having to give up on my future plans. I shared my concern with a friend who was a camp director in the area. He told me that a camp on an adjacent lake, called Camp Hawthorne, had recently closed, and that the camp's owners might be interested in selling their business to me, but I would first need to get the family who owned the land and buildings to allow me to take over the existing twelve-year lease on the camp property.

It was much easier than I expected to win over the confidence of the Plummer family, who owned the land and buildings, and be approved to take over the lease. I might have been their only option at the time. It was a leap of faith on my part that I would be able to pay the rent on the lease and insurance on the property for a minimum of twelve years. I was also responsible for maintenance and repairs for over twenty buildings—all in disrepair.

The business, which had closed, was selling its camp equipment for $32,000, which included sailboats, canoes, a motorboat, camp beds, kitchen equipment, and dining room furniture. I had only $4,000 in savings to go toward the purchase of the equipment. It was decided that would be my first year's payment. I would have four years to get the camp up and running and pay off the balance of my note.

In addition to the note, the sizable lease, which included the property taxes on two-and-a-half miles of prime shorefront, was structured so that the rent would not be due until May of each year. Hopefully I would have enough children enrolled for the coming summer to cover all my expenses. Providence seemed to be on my side. Whatever obstacle I faced along the way, someone stepped forward to help me.

The following stories are about Camp Hawthorne. Portions of these stories have been published in the American Camping Association's *Camping Magazine*. "Back to Basics," "Jason's Story," and "The Guardian Angel" were published in my first book, *The Bait Store and Other Stories*.

Back to Basics

~~~~~~~

I have always enjoyed telling campfire stories at camp. It was the favorite part of my job as director of Camp Hawthorne. Memories rush to mind when I think back to those extraordinary evenings—the warm hush that surrounded the gathering, the crackling and smell of the pine wood fire, and so many dirty feet. The campers would huddle together, eager to hear their favorite story from a summer past, less enthusiastic to work their way through a new story never told before. It was as if they waited all winter to return to camp for this gathering alone, to again be together among the tall pines on the edge of Panther Pond. Our campfire site was their Stonehenge, holy ground to most of these little earthly travelers. It was my job to help produce the magic.

At the end of each camp session, on what we called Pickup Day, parents were always astonished at the difficulty their children would have separating from camp and piling into the family car for the return trip home. Bunkmates would hug each other, sobbing as they said good-bye to new friendships woven out of the fabric of camp life. Some of these suburban parents had previously spent endless hours arranging play dates with cousins and neighbors and engineering appropriate friendships for their children. How could three weeks of living together in the rundown shanty town called Camp Hawthorne affect their children so deeply?

Some parents probed for answers from their children on the ride home. The talkative ones shared endless stories about camp life—night talks with their counselors, new friends who felt like brothers or sisters, and, especially, camp silliness. Parents who listened patiently to their children would soon uncover the truth about life at camp. It wasn't what their children *did* at camp that was most important, it was how they *felt* at camp that gave the experience its power.

Few people would disagree that we now live in a world of consumer capitalism. Our open lands and lakefronts in New England are slowly disappearing to development. Many young children are overstimulated and overscheduled. This generation, more than any other in our history, needs the calming and regenerative powers of living close to the natural rhythms and flow of nature.

Overnight camps first appeared in New England around 1900. Camps were started by a host of individuals who had prior careers as doctors, teachers, school guidance counselors, and college and high school coaches.

While land was considerably less expensive back then, these pioneers in camping relied on bank mortgages, friends, and family to provide seed money for what must have felt like a risky enterprise. Most camps had rustic buildings and sports fields that had recently been cow pastures. Amenities such as tennis courts, electricity, and hot showers were nonexistent. As the camping industry grew and competition became brisk, many camps moved away from their simple roots and developed into facilities that resembled resorts.

I have always felt that the value of a camp experience lies in taking campers out of their suburban or urban comfort zones and sharing the power of living close to nature in simple surroundings.

Back in 1918, the founder of Camp Hawthorne, Major Bigelow, searched the entire state of Maine for the perfect lakeside property to begin his camping business. He came across a small farm on the edge of Panther Pond. With over two miles of shorefront and a mile of sandy beach with fields and woodlands, it was what many believed to be the most beautiful beachfront property in the state. And Camp Hawthorne was born.

An owner of the farm property, David Plummer, built the cabins and dining hall that still stand today. The cabins were simple structures perched on a knoll overlooking the lake. Amazingly, the structures, hardly more substantial than a chicken coop, had survived the harsh Maine winters.

When I took over the lease of the camp in 1988,

I was concerned that the rustic look of the camp buildings might be off-putting to some parents and/or campers. What I soon discovered was that from the children's point of view, the simple, lived-in construction of the property helped them feel more invested in the camp as their summer home.

Maybe the cabins reminded the campers of an old fort or clubhouse they built themselves with friends in their hometown neighborhood. Maybe they felt they could have built their cabins themselves with some hand tools and a box of nails.

Many of the supporting beams of the cabins were signed and dated with the names of prior campers going back as far as 1919. Campers could lie on their cots, read the names, and imagine what camp was like back then. The buildings were far from perfect, but they seemed to have a soul of their own and an aura of contentment.

A camp setting should feel like a little village where everyone knows each other by name and children are free to move around the camp perimeter with only limited restrictions under the supervision of caring adults.

Our camp was a good match for the sensibilities of the children. They could secretly add their own name on the underside of a window frame and no one minded. A projectile could pierce a hole in a screen door and, with a little duct tape, could be repaired without punishment. Each day tons of sand would be transported from the beach into the bunk on dirty feet, to be recycled and swept out the door the following morning.

Evening campfires were a sacred time at camp. Our campfire site was situated at the edge of the lake, which gave us a perfect view of the moon rising over the water. We sat on old logs surrounding the fire pit and burned pine branches we all collected from the woods. With the campfire lighting up their faces, campers eagerly waited to hear their favorite camp stories and for the camp musicians to play and lead us in familiar songs.

Once a week, each cabin group hiked to their own special fire pit carrying food and water for a meal they would prepare themselves over an open fire. Campers sought out the perfect stick to roast a hot dog or sausage. It would be easy to imagine how their ancestors would sit by a similar fire to cook and hear the oral traditions of their people.

Canoeing down a river, sailing on a windy afternoon, climbing a mountain, learning archery, and tree fort building are all camp activities that have stood the test of time and deserve to be passed on to today's youth. Living close to nature, relying on one's own imagination to entertain oneself and friends, learning to tolerate feelings of moderate anxiety from separating from home, living cooperatively with others, and developing an independent sense of oneself are experiences that strengthen the souls of our children.

Summer camp has always supported the psychological growth of children. Living simply and communally in a rustic, natural setting away from the pressures of school life and the distractions of mass media can both comfort and strengthen the foundation of children's emerging sense of self. Nature is a wonderful healer of the soul. We all need to connect to the natural world whenever possible. Nothing fancy is needed—when it comes to camp, rustic is sometimes just what our children crave.

A Rather Odd Addiction

The snowstorm only added to my anxiety as I made my way up the Maine turnpike to Bath, Maine. I was due at three o'clock at the lawyer's office of the owners of Camp Hawthorne to sign the legal documents that would turn the camp corporation over to me. I had already secured a twelve-year lease on the land and buildings. Now I needed to purchase the existing camp corporation and make my first payment on a list of camp equipment, which I had never actually seen.

My personal funds did not allow me to bring legal counsel to this meeting. I had previously met with a lawyer for just an hour for some advice, only to decide to do my own legal work. I brought some documents that I had written for them to sign, even though I knew they would have little chance of protecting me in court if I was to inherit any liability by taking over their existing corporation. I didn't have the funds to create a new corporation that would have given me real protection from any legal problems stemming from the past operation of the camp. I had already figured the whole experience of taking responsibility for this failing camp was a total leap of faith, so why stop now?

The couple selling the corporation was waiting for me with their lawyer when I arrived a few minutes late. No one offered me coffee. Legal papers were quickly shuffled around for signatures. I didn't know enough about what I was doing to even ask any questions. The room felt as icy as the weather outside. I wondered if they thought I was a naïve idiot.

The lawyer said, "Well, then, you are now the new owner of Camp Hawthorne." With that pronouncement, the seller handed me a ring of keys to all the buildings, gates, and storage cupboards at the camp. None of the keys were marked as to what door or lock they belonged to. There must have been a hundred. Some were skeleton keys, others looked like keys to old farm tractors. Nothing looked familiar, like a normal house key. They were all dangling from a circular key ring that made me think they belonged to the warden at Sing Sing Prison.

My anxiety by now was going through the roof, and I was sure everyone in the room knew it. I felt a full-fledged panic attack coming on. Please God, not now. I asked to be pointed in the direction of the rest room. When I opened the door to the bathroom I could hear the radiator hissing away. It must have been ninety degrees in there, which just added to the mounting pressure in my head.

Being handed that ring of keys to buildings I knew nothing about was clearly the cause of my overload. Was I crazy? I had no right putting my family in potential financial ruin by buying a camp I had looked at for less than an hour on a snowy day in January. I hoped splashing cold water on my face would help me calm down.

I returned to the meeting a few minutes later and attempted to cover up my state of mind. Somehow, in the time I was gone, the tone in the room had changed. The wife of the couple spoke for the first time. She had been a nurse. Maybe she had worked in mental hospitals.

She acknowledged that I must be overwhelmed with my new responsibility. She said she had felt that way herself when they had taken over the camp eight years earlier. She said that they would be available to help me learn the ropes and would surely help me open up the camp in May. They had bought a house on the lake not far from the camp and often made the trip across the lake to enjoy the sun on our south-facing sandy beach. They also volunteered their two sons to help; both grew up at the camp and were heading to engineering colleges.

Her husband then told me that the water system was complicated and finicky. Camp drinking water came from an old well dug back in 1919. The toilets and laundry used chlorinated lake water that also ran to each building. He assured me that for at least the first year and maybe longer, he and his old camp buddies would help me learn how to both put on the water system in the spring and shut it down in the fall.

I couldn't feel more grateful. Maybe I could learn these new skills? Growing up Jewish in a suburb of Boston offered a young college-bound boy few opportunities to learn hands-on trades like plumbing, electrical work, basic construction, and maintenance. I owned only a few tools, and they were for simple bicycle repair.

Within a few seasons of operating the camp, I managed to learn enough skills to keep licensed plumbers, electricians, and roofers off my meager payroll. I felt quite proud that I could repair most of the everyday emergencies that could otherwise shut down a summer camp operation. I loved trying to figure out a better way to keep my camp operating like a well-oiled machine. Whenever I was forced to hire a tradesman to repair or replace something, I would try to assist the workman and ask a million questions so I could learn the secrets of the trades.

Before I became a camp director, I worked as a psychotherapist at a mental health clinic near my home. Once the camp became stable enough to support my family, I shortened my therapy practice to a few days a week and suspended it for the eight weeks of camp.

One afternoon the clinical director, Dr. Waters, talked to me about a client she wanted me to see on a weekly basis. His name was David, and he worked at a company that manufactured chrome parts for the auto industry. David suffered from a rare and unclassified addiction; a compulsion to travel to the local Sears department store every weekend to purchase appliances and electronic equipment that he didn't need. I was told his house was jammed, with three or more washing machines, clothes dryers, humidifiers, dehumidifiers, freezers, and an assortment of television sets, CB and short wave radios, ship-to-shore radios, scanners, five electric razors, six electric knives—well, you get the picture.

David, now fifty-seven years old, was the adopted child of a well-respected Boston family. His father, long deceased, had been a superior court justice for Massachusetts. He knew David would need financial support in his life, so money was left for David's care that was controlled by a trustee at State Street Bank. The trustee would periodically bail David and his wife out of financial ruin. The trustee contacted our clinic to see if we could help David control his impulsive behaviors and stop making purchases at Sears that he clearly didn't need or use.

My first meeting with David was uneventful. He filled my four o'clock slot and came directly from work. David always wore blue work shirts and pants. His hair was thinning and disheveled. He showed little emotional affect, which I soon learned was due to an overload of electro-shock treatments administered to him during his long stay at a Massachusetts mental hospital. David had met his wife at the hospital. They had been married for over twenty years.

I always found it dreadfully difficult staying alert for my four o'clock therapy appointments. My energy was at low ebb, and all I could think about was a mid day nap. Seeing David for therapy at this time posed great challenges for me. I kept a plug-in percolator full of coffee in my office because I believed it was a nice gesture to offer clients coffee when they arrived for therapy. I would need three cups of strong black coffee to get through my hour with David.

David was able to share some of his personal history, speaking in short sentences. I would begin our session by asking him about trips to Sears. He offered no rational explanation for his compulsive behaviors. I once had his wife join him for therapy. She cried through the entire hour while David looked on with a blank expression. As one might imagine, this was one long hour.

I liked David and wanted to find a way to help him. David drove to therapy in a Toyota van. The roof of the van sported six antennas connecting David to a wide range of electronics. When I spotted an additional antenna on his van, I knew he had bought something new at Sears. Thank God—that would give me something new to discuss with him. My personal modality as a therapist was to develop trust and unconditional positive regard toward my clients. I was a firm follower of the work of Dr. Carl Rogers. I knew David had no personal friends and rarely spent time with family, other than his wife. I decided to find a way to develop a meaningful relationship with him.

If David was capable of hooking up an array of electronic gear in his car, he must have some skills I didn't have. Each year I faced new challenges as I tried to keep Camp Hawthorne from collapsing. Maybe David could help me plan my camp's building projects for the coming summer. Now, I know it could sound self-serving to use David's therapy time in this way, especially, since I was being paid for the hour. However, this would give something for David and me to talk about each week, and it might develop into a meaningful relationship for him.

I checked out my idea with Dr. Waters. She agreed it was worth a try. Each week I thought up new projects to ask David to help me plan. He seemed to get pleasure in trying to help me with his ideas. On many occasions, his ideas were better than mine. He enjoyed helping me, and it seemed that both of us were looking forward to our four o'clock meetings. Our meetings went on for almost four years. I felt David was learning how to have a friend. By this time David had twelve antennas fastened to the roof of his car.

I was informed that the clinic was going to change its operations. I would no longer be able to see clients in the Boston office. This was a relief to me, since the camp was prospering, and I no longer had the time for my trips to Boston. It was decided that Dr. Waters would take on David as her client.

Around two weeks after I terminated my therapy sessions with David, I got a call from Dr. Waters. She was eager to share with me her experience with David. She said David showed up for his first meeting with a very sad look on his face. She thought he was about to cry. When she asked him what was wrong, he said he was worried about Ron. When she asked him why he was worried about me. David replied, "that poor man doesn't know how to do anything!!"

Providence Is On My Side

I have always felt there was a streak of good luck that followed me in the re-creation and operation of Camp Hawthorne. I believed it was the result of years of developing a positive image in my mind of what a camp of my making would look and feel like. At the age of thirty-eight, I committed myself to moving ahead with plans that only existed as flashes of images in my mind. My intuition then led me to the places and people that actualized what I always believed would be my path in life.

I tried to share my feeling that Providence was somehow on my side with staff working with me at camp. Some saw evidence of it while others thought I was full of crap. I remember an incident that happened in early June one summer when my assistant director and I were driving back to camp from the lumberyard in rural Maine.

We were discussing the possibility of putting a

diving board on one of our floats at the waterfront. We had inherited a fiberglass diving board with the old camp equipment, but were missing the hardware to attach it to its metal frame. We decided that we needed two thick metal brackets designed to fit the board with holes drilled into it so it could be attached to the frame. At just that moment, we drove past a small commercial building with a sign that read "Machine Shop."

I immediately pulled into their driveway and said to my passenger that they would be eager to help us. He responded by trying to convince me that one can't just walk into an unknown business and convince everyone to stop whatever they were doing and recalibrate their machinery to make two quarter-inch-thick steel brackets for a camp toy.

It took some convincing to get him to follow me into the factory building. I think he was embarrassed for me and afraid I might be showing signs of early dementia. We entered the building and were quickly led into the office of the owner. I said I could see how busy he was and didn't expect that he could help us, but nonetheless we had this idea of how we could assemble a diving board for our summer campers.

Somehow I captured his imagination. He led us into the factory and to his designer who drew up a picture of the brackets he thought we needed. Within minutes four different machine shop operators were cutting out the metal pieces, bending them to our specifications, drilling the holes that were needed and polishing the brackets to make sure there were no sharp edges that could hurt anyone. No one complained in any way that our project was interfering with them getting their regular work done. They were somehow all on board and seemed to be delighted in helping us. Within fifteen minutes we were out the door after I paid a meager bill of only fifteen dollars.

This type of Providence was particularly evident on a trip I ran for twenty older campers some years ago. I designed a fourteen-day camping adventure that would take us to many of my favorite places and hidden gems in Maine. We would climb mountains, swim in pristine rivers, canoe, and ocean kayak, and just explore Maine's spectacular landscapes from the coastal towns of Stonington and Lubec to the western mountains in the Rangeley Lakes district.

We traveled in two new passenger vans plus a 1986 Chevy van I owned in which we carried all our clothing, sleeping bags, cooking gear, tents, food, and ice chests. A trusted former staff member named Chris was willing to come along and drive the cargo van for no salary since he suspected our trip would be something he didn't want to miss.

One destination took us into Canada to visit Campobello Island and the summer home of President and Eleanor Roosevelt. We had just explored the ocean cliffs of Quoddy Head State Park and got a late start as we crossed a steep one-lane bridge from Lubec, Maine, into Canada.

On our return trip we were held up on top of the bridge while we waited our turn to go through American customs. The van stalled, and when Chris attempted to restart it, the engine would not respond. I thought Chris was playing a joke on me when he ran up to my van to tell me the news. I ran back with him and tried to start the van myself. It appeared the engine starter was no longer functioning.

I had to think fast because our broken down van was actually keeping other cars from entering the United States. The cargo van remained stuck on the bridge while I took my turn at customs. I frantically explained to the customs agent our precarious situation.

I ran up the bridge to our stalled van with four of my staff. Our only option was to try to push the van to customs. Since we were holding up many other cars on the bridge, some strangers joined us in pushing the van the 500 feet or so to get it off the bridge. I struggled with the steering to keep it on the road and not damage the bridge or ourselves.

When I returned to the customs office, a very cordial officer came immediately to our aid. He said he had already called a tow truck for us and was about to make reservations for our group at a local campground. He could see we were incapable of continuing our trip without the van that transported all our equipment. One does not expect a customs agent to go out of his way to help a group like ours.

The agent told me he once had this problem with

an old Chevy van like mine. He also thought the trouble was the starter and felt that if he could crawl under the van and smash the casing of the starter just right, the solenoid might release, which could give us one last start. The tow truck had already arrived when my new friend expertly hammered the starter and, like magic, the engine started.

The tow truck driver followed us to the campground to drop off all our gear before we headed to his garage where I hoped he could somehow fix us up with a new starter. It was already past seven in the evening and I knew the campers would be starving. When the tow truck driver said we were going to his garage, I did not understand that he meant the garage at his home. There were no other repair shops in town. How could he fix the van, since I never saw a lift in his small garage?

I was pondering my predicament while driving back to the campground. How is this guy going to find a starter for my 1986 Chevy van way up on the Canadian border? I was helpless and didn't even have cell phone coverage. We most likely would be stuck at the campground for days if not longer. I feared that a new starter might have to come from Detroit where the van was made.

I spent a sleepless night trying to figure out my next move. Around five in the morning it started to rain. We had no shelter so I assumed we would have to eat breakfast in the rain. How would I entertain my group of twenty adolescent boys and girls if we faced many days stuck at this campground? At around seven I couldn't stand lying around my tent any longer. I was not even certain I could find the home of the man working on my van since I paid little attention to his location when I dropped it off.

I could not believe it when I saw our van parked in front of the man's home. How could he move it from his garage without it being fixed? I dropped it off at seven in the evening. It was now a little after seven the next morning.

I slowly walked up to the front door feeling sheepish about showing up so early. He must have seen me coming and met me behind the screen door. I stated I was sorry to bother him so early but I was interested to know if he had any ideas of how to get hold of a starter for my van. He just smiled at me and said, "the van was fixed by six this morning."

"How is that possible?" I asked, "I thought we needed a new starter."

"Well," he said, "I was looking in an old pile of junk in the garage last night and came across a new starter I must have ordered for someone twenty years ago who never showed up."

As it turned out, it was exactly what he needed to get me going. The price on the box was only forty dollars in 1991 so that was all he charged me for the part. Back on the road heading to our campsite I felt a deep wave of relief rocket through my body. Providence was again on my side.

Camp Silliness

S illiness was a main ingredient of Camp Hawthorne philosophy. As a camp that encouraged creativity among our campers and staff, fun was bound to creep in at any moment, transforming camp life into a circus of silliness.

A typical day at Camp Hawthorne began with a wake-up call at 7:45 followed by breakfast and cabin cleanup. The first period, called our major period, began at 9:30. This was our longest period of the day where campers sign up for an activity they wished to focus on for a full week. Campers could make new choices at the beginning of each week. Our most popular choices were water-skiing, sailing, creative writing, and stained glass. Counselors were also encouraged to come up with other creative choices to offer the campers.

One summer we added a new bathroom at the end of our bathhouse. The bathroom was roughed in and operational but unfinished, as a new camp session began. Adam, one of our more visionary and silly counselors, came to me with an idea for major period. He wanted to offer bathroom beautification. It was true that our existing bathrooms needed a face-lift. Adam was convinced he could pull it off and that I would love the new bathroom once it was completed.

Adam's proposal sounded like one of the stupidest ideas I had heard in a while, which was saying a lot at our camp. However, I didn't want to dampen his enthusiasm so I agreed to offer it at our signup meeting. If he could get six campers to commit, he was on. I did challenge him by limiting his budget to fifty dollars of camp money for the project. His instincts proved correct; over fifteen campers signed up for bathroom beautification as their first choice for the weeklong major period.

After meeting with the campers for their first day of planning, Adam and his crew came up with an idea. They wanted to keep it a secret, even from me. Adam promised me that what they were doing was going to be a multimedia event. I was a little nervous, but I trusted Adam and gave my approval. Everyone on the team was now in a frenzy to transform our bathroom.

One of the older campers Adam attracted to his project was named Daniel. His mother told me, when he first came to camp, that Daniel was probably the most intelligent person I would ever meet in my life. Daniel was a theoretical thinker who seemed to have advanced knowledge of electronics. I noticed him hanging around the camp office, designing circuitry for the bathroom, so I gave him permission to call home and check out his ideas with his father. I was worried he might blow up the camp.

The camp was buzzing with anticipation around the new bathroom. I was instructed to stay away until the project was completed and unveiled to the whole community. Some of Adam's campers rushed into the office each morning when the mail was delivered in search of a special package, the contents of which was held to be top secret. When the package finally arrived, it was whisked off by the campers.

On the day of the unveiling, a writer from the *Bostonia Magazine*, an alumni magazine of Boston University, arrived to visit the camp to write a story. Adam had tipped her off to come to his presentation. A red ribbon stretched across the bathroom door. Although I trusted Adam, I feared what we were about to see.

The ribbon was cut and Adam's campers beamed with delight as Adam described their creative project—a disco bathroom. Their inspiration came from the dance floor in the movie *Saturday Night Fever*. The floor was painted in a checkerboard pattern with twelve-inch squares of red, green, and black. The walls were brightly painted with stenciled borders depicting John Travolta in his classic dance move with his right arm shot up into the air.

Adam announced, "Now for the big surprise." With a flick of the light switch, the bathroom transformed into

a disco dance hall. A disco ball—the secret package—
hung from the ceiling and began to turn and reflect the
colored lights that shone onto it. Strings of red and white
Christmas lights started to blink to the Bee Gees' hit,
"Staying Alive," part of the *Saturday Night Fever* sound
track.

The camp community roared with delight. The
writer for the magazine was duly impressed and made
our disco bathroom the focal point of her story.

Silliness permeated our life at Camp Hawthorne.
It lifted our spirits, brought the community together in
a spirit of fun, connected everyone to their inner child,
and encouraged the expression of our thespian selves. All
that was needed was a well- stocked costume room, a few
props and a culture of joyful play.

Camp Chapel

R eligious education directors of many branches of organized religion struggle to develop programs to affect the inner life of children. Many exist with the main purpose of offering a Sunday/Saturday religious education program for children during religious services, so that parents can join other adults in the main sanctuary for religious worship. Some are committed to teaching religious doctrine and customs leading up to a confirmation experience or rite of passage into adult life.

Most of these programs exist in the midst of an adult world in large impressive buildings, taught by adults with specific goals in mind.

Religion teachers and parent volunteers feel great satisfaction in helping young souls become members of a God-fearing society. However, in my experience in talking to many children about their religious education, many feel their real job is pleasing their parents, not discovering a spiritual connection for themselves.

The rustic, natural setting of a children's resident summer camp provides a better environment for creating a spiritual place for children. A simple chapel in the woods surrounded by a lake, trees, birds, and wildlife is a more believable place of worship for children. The setting can be as simple as one the campers themselves might construct with a few hand tools and a group of friends.

Every Sunday morning at Camp Hawthorne—after bunkhouse cleanup was completed—campers and counselors from each of our eleven cabins would make their way to our chapel in the woods. The ten-minute walk to chapel wove its way down a narrow trail by the lake. We all walked in silence. Everyone knew this was a special time. We walked to a spot in the woods by the lake that felt sacred to our camp community because of the energy that was created during the service.

Our entire community of campers, counselors, kitchen workers, nurses, and teaching staff were eager to make it to chapel on time. It was rare that Mother Nature did not provide the perfect morning. We sat on logs impersonating church pews on a small hill that allowed everyone a view of the lake. The morning sun reflected light off the lake and onto the overhanging leaves of the maple and birch trees that surrounded us.

Once everyone arrived and settled in, I led a group meditation that began with rhythmic breathing, followed by visualizing energy as a stream of white light moving up from deep inside the earth and filling the space of our bodies. We then visualized this stream of white light leaving our bodies at the crown of our heads and surrounding us in an imaginary egg of white light. I reminded them that surrounding themselves in an aura of light would help them feel protected and rejuvenated. Visualizing an aura of white light is a common ritual used by many spiritual communities around the world. We then imagined our individual auras expanding to surround the entire camp community, then to encompass all the people and cultures of the earth.

The camp community gently returned to the present moment as I softly played a Native American flute. Over the years, many campers have shared with me that our meditations helped them relax, feel grounded, and connect to a positive and protective energy they could tap in to. Following the September 11th attacks, I received numerous emails from campers who said they used our meditation to feel comforted and to lessen their anxiety.

Children respond best to simple rituals that provide immediate results. An outdoor group meditation or visualization done correctly can create a feeling of warmth and love that children can feel. Children, like adults in our society, need to be drawn out of their heads and into their bodies and senses. They respond well to visualizations that raise their thoughts and inner consciousness to a place of love and peacefulness. Traditional religious worship can accomplish similar results through rituals (communion in Christianity; opening the ark housing the Torah in

Judaism), but such rituals are not always able to affect the inner life of children. Children do best when the service is geared to them.

Following the meditation, our chapel service transforms into a kind of Quaker Friends meeting, where campers are given an opportunity to thank other campers and staff who have helped them in their adjustment to camp life. Campers and staff would rise to speak individually to thank others in the community who had helped them in some way. Returning campers, used to sharing gratitude, acted as models for newer, younger campers.

First year campers are often scared and anxious when they first leave home to come to camp. The chapel service supported and welcomed these new campers. Since all of our camp sessions began on a Saturday, the Sunday chapel services fell on the first full day of camp, which can be a fertile time for homesickness to appear.

All children experience some anxiety when they arrive at camp. Once they hear other campers talk about their fears, homesickness, or concerns about making friends and being accepted, they understand that their feelings are a natural part of adjusting to camp. It was not uncommon for a camper to talk about personal pain, knowing the community would support him. Some asked for forgiveness for having acted unkindly.

I believe that camp provides an excellent opportunity to develop the important skills needed to lead a healthy and productive life. One such skill is learning to tolerate anxiety without retreating to safe and familiar ground. Our modern society can move too quickly to protect children when what many need is to learn how to stay focused when facing moderate anxiety. A healthy separation from home and adjusting to be part of a dynamic camp community can offer the perfect setting to develop those skills as long as caring and sensitive adults are present to help mentor the process.

Our service then turned to sharing personal insights campers had learned while at camp. I was always impressed when campers shared new ways of seeing themselves. Many spoke of how different they feel at camp from how they feel at school, where many felt you needed to look or act a certain way to be accepted. At camp, if you are just yourself, you feel your worth to the community. There was no shortage of wisdom to be shared with everyone.

Following the time of sharing, I often talked with them for a few minutes on three themes:

1. **Gratitude.** I encouraged them to practice gratitude on a daily basis, and to write home to thank their parents for the opportunity of coming to camp.

2. **Happy memories.** I spoke about the importance of having happy childhood memories as a foundation for the rest of their lives. Camp is not a place to worry about dating, world problems, or how their parents are getting

along without them. Camp is a place to enjoy childhood in all its innocence, joy, silliness, and fun. I urged them to resist the pressure to grow up too fast because they would miss out on the fun in life.

3. **The mysteries of life.** I reminded campers that camp is a place where extraordinary experiences often happen. By keeping hearts open to the mysteries that surround them and minds receptive to new ways of thinking, they could deepen their appreciation of life.

Sunday service concluded with the singing of our chapel song, "Give Yourself to Love," by Kate Wolf and followed by my reading an original camp blessing. Campers take their time exiting the chapel area as hugs and smiles are warmly exchanged.

Our camp attracted campers and staff from all religious and ethnic backgrounds. The combined community might define themselves as Jewish, Christian, Unitarian, Muslim, or atheist, so our service needed to reach everyone in a meaningful way. A service oriented toward nature, with a Quaker style of sharing insights and feelings when moved to speak, proved a successful way to include everyone. The visualization focusing on inner light was accessible to all. The chapel experience was sacred to us because we used the sacred time and space to feel close to the creative power of nature. The concept of sacred time and space expanded to include our campfires, where music and storytelling became other tools to create the same outcome as chapel.

On the second-to-last night of each camp session, campers were given the opportunity to be part of our Native American–style sweat lodge. Two cabins of campers at a time who wished to take part in the sweat lodge, left the campfire with their counselors and waited silently on the ball field by the lake while campers who chose not to take part remained at the campfire to listen to stories.

To get ready for the lodge, the older campers had collected large rocks and firewood from dead trees in the forest. A bonfire was built and rocks were placed around it and heated for three hours. The lodge, a circular tent, was built out of tarps and wood poles.

The ceremony began when the heated rocks were brought into the lodge and placed in a round pit in the center. The heat and steam were controlled by the number of hot rocks, their placement in the pit, and the amount of water poured over them. Campers entered with their counselors after waiting on the ball field. A senior staff member whom we called the Guardian of the Lodge and who had experience running sweat lodges, performed a short ceremony with the ritual herb sage.

Campers were given time to share their most personal feelings about their camp experience with their group. The ceremony lasted twenty minutes and concluded with special songs and chants related to the sweat lodge. After each group took a quick dip in the lake to further cool down, they walked silently back to their cabins with the counselors.

Our sweat lodge was carefully supervised, and campers could leave the lodge at any time. I offered this experience for each of our three camp sessions for twenty-four summers without a problem. Many campers said it was the high point of their summer.

The very nature of the rustic camp experience is magical. Hearing the call of the loons on a lake, sitting around a campfire to listen to stories, and seeing the night sky lit up with stars just adds to that wonder. Creating sacred time at camp through experiences like our camp chapel, campfires, and sweat lodge makes the camp experience even more rewarding.

Jason's Story

❧

Whenever a parent called with an interest in our camp for a child diagnosed with Asperger's syndrome, I asked to meet with the family beforehand to make certain that he or she could have a successful adjustment to camp. Jason's family heard about us through a camp referral service. His mom told me that her eleven-year-old son was a musically precocious and gifted child. His father was a musician with a renowned symphony orchestra, so I assumed Jason's innate talents were encouraged or at least inherited from his dad.

I set out to meet Jason on a snowy morning with my wife, a teacher, and our two young sons; the forecasted weather had granted them a rare snow day off from school. By 10:00, however, the weather had changed, so we felt we could make the trip with little difficulty.

Jason's mother greeted us warmly when we arrived

and directed us to the den to wait for Jason, but Jason didn't appear. He refused to come down from the upstairs landing and shouted for us to go away. I could see that my two children were going to enjoy this show of power, as Jason's mother tried every imaginable trick to bring him downstairs. After ten minutes of verbal combat with his mother, I thought I might be able to break the ice by sitting on the bottom stairs with his mom and looking at brightly colored pictures from our camp album that showed the camp's setting and activities that campers most enjoyed.

By a stroke of luck, we came across a picture of a rainy-day activity in which we set up the dining hall to resemble a gambling casino. The counselors man tables for blackjack, poker, and roulette. Campers get small amounts of penny candy for their winnings. "Look, Jason," his mother said, "they have gambling at Hawthorne." Like a magic word, the idea of gambling unlocked any resistance Jason was having of going to camp. "Let me look," he said as he hurtled down the stairs to see for himself. Was this true, did Hawthorne really have gambling?

I took the liberty of exaggerating the extent to which gambling was an integral part of the camp program, with the good intention of helping Jason open up to the possibility of a new adventure at sleepaway camp. My wife and I immediately realized we had to have Jason at camp. He was wholly endearing. You could not help but love this boy at first sight. My children were not quite as positive, but felt better when they realized that Jason was not of an age that would put him in either of their bunkhouses at camp.

Jason arrived at camp and had little difficulty separating from his parents. He insisted that he be allowed to wear headphones and carry his portable tape player. This was breaking camp rules, but an exception that seemed reasonable to accommodate. We later realized that Jason brought only one tape—of the musical *Carousel*—which he listened to throughout the day. He was, after all, coming to Maine for camp—the coast of Maine being the setting for the musical.

Jason adjusted so well that we decided in the first week he could remain at camp for the whole summer. In fact, Jason came to camp for the full season for the next six summers. We had to adjust his schedule for his quirky behaviors, like setting aside time to make sand castles on the beach while listening to *Carousel* on his tape player.

Jason's hygiene was not much better than a feral child's. He fought to wear a favorite red-and-blue-striped shirt each day. On laundry day I threatened to make him walk through a car wash with it on if he would not put it in his laundry bag. Meanwhile, Jason's camp cubby had many carefully folded outfits sent by his mother, as if he were heading for a golf tournament.

Jason had perfect pitch, a natural gift of many musicians. Whenever a bell went off, a horn sounded, or a telephone rang, Jason would throw up his hands and yell out what key the sound was anchored in. He assured me ten thousand times that the camp office phone was ringing squarely in B flat.

Jason could never be rushed and needed adequate warning time for any schedule change. His sense of self would become disorganized and frantic whenever we attempted to move him too quickly into a camp van for a trip to the beach or a camping or canoe trip. He would seek me out, believing that I was behind this unsettling change of events, and shout, "We are not in rockets, Ron!"

On Jason's fifth summer at camp we discovered one of his most bizarre behaviors. Jason appeared to prefer foraging for food in barrels and dumpsters than picking it up cafeteria style in our dining room. I had allowed a local company to hold a picnic and lobster bake for their employees on our ball field and insisted that they bring their own dumpster so the lobster waste would not bake in the sun and stink up the camp.

The following morning, before their dumpster got hauled away, we discovered Jason had gotten up at dawn and climbed into the dumpster to forage for leftover morsels of lobster meat. When Jason arrived at the dining room for morning announcements, it was clear that he had gotten into something very smelly indeed. Tiny pieces of decaying lobster meat hung from his face and cheeks. When I confronted him about why he thought diving in a dumpster was a normal camp activity, Jason just smiled his infectious smile and exclaimed, "How else do you expect me to get any real Maine food around here?" He was quickly forgiven and sent to the showers while I set his tee shirt on fire. I wondered if this strange behavior might have been encouraged by his constant listening to the *Carousel* music, which featured a song about a wonderful Maine clambake.

Jason gave me the pleasure one evening of making me laugh so hard I thought I would need to be taken to a hospital to catch my breath. My fit of laughter was prompted during one of our camp talent shows where campers share their most extraordinary talents. Yes, there was the occasional piano or flute recital, but more often it was a chance to take the stage and show how you can take a piece of spaghetti and stick it up you nose and then have it exit your mouth—always a camp crowd pleaser.

To everyone's surprise, Jason took the stage and told us he was going to act out a complete episode of *The Simpsons*—a popular TV show—playing every character and even making the sounds of the opening music. By now our camp community was so in love with this camper that his antics delighted us all. No one was laughing at Jason, everyone was laughing with him. He jumped all over the stage, assuming the characters in rapid succession. The lodge roared with delight at his expressiveness and humor.

Our camp community cherished the atypical campers who were attracted to our summer programs. Many of these children were poorly equipped to create personal best friends at school or home, but at camp, with the structure and routine of camp life, they could feel part of a ready-made group of peers. These campers had a particular charm about them because they were so real. They lacked the pretense, bragging, or competitive angst you often see in early adolescent children. Their blunt honesty about their needs and feelings helped us make Camp Hawthorne a place where all campers felt free to be themselves. These individuals still hold a place deep in my heart and in my camp memories. I miss them terribly even now, years after they moved on.

Cara's Story

O ne winter morning I received a call at home from a mother of one of our campers who wanted to talk about the possibility of her daughter enrolling in Camp Hawthorne the following summer. The mother, named Eve, was up front that her daughter had psychological and developmental issues due to her birth mother's struggles with addiction. Eve said her daughter, Cara, had been placed in foster care at birth, and shortly after joined their family of three children. Cara was soon adopted by the family and was now eight years old.

Eve said she could certainly understand if I was unwilling to accept a child at camp who could present so many challenges to the camp community. Her son was enrolled to return to camp for his second summer. He was an outstanding camper who loved our relaxed and spirited camp environment. Eve stated that if her daughter was ever to go to camp, we offered the best chance for her to succeed. I told her I would keep an open mind. We scheduled a meeting at my home the following weekend.

When they arrived, I immediately noticed that Cara and her mother had a similar appearance. One could be easily convinced that her adopted mother was her birth mother. They were both slight in figure, had similar pixie-style short haircuts and both looked like they would have been uncomfortable wearing a dress. Cara sat close to her mother as I gently showed them pictures from our camp album. Fortunately, I was able to point out pictures of her brother laughing with his friends and enjoying camp activities.

The meeting went as well as one could expect. Cara was clingy and showed some signs of emotional distress. She appeared to act more like a five-year-old than an eight-year-old girl. She did seem to make a connection to me by leaning against me when we looked at the camp picture album together as I explained a typical day at camp. Eve felt the meeting went well, and stated that Cara could think about what she learned on the ride back to the city.

I was floored when Eve called that evening to tell me that Cara asked her many questions in the car and actually sounded as if she was going to be at Camp Hawthorne for the upcoming summer. Cara's mother impressed me with her commitment and sensitivity toward her daughter. I assured her that if Cara were to change her mind, even on the opening day of camp, I would surely return her full tuition. I wanted both of them to understand that we were all in this together.

Cara arrived with her older brother on the opening day of camp. I had placed Cara in our youngest cabin of girls with a counselor who, I felt, had the heart and maturity to provide Cara with the best chance of success. Her counselor's name was also Cara, which gave them both a good starting point. I advised Eve to make her parting with Cara short and sweet, since prolonged goodbyes often make separation more difficult.

Little Cara followed her big counselor Cara around camp like a baby duckling following her mother. We tried to arrange their camp schedules so that they were never far apart. She was as cute as a little camper could be and everyone in the camp community rejoiced in her success—with the possible exception of some of the young campers in her cabin who rightly felt that Cara was receiving way too much attention.

Cara had one behavior that seriously concerned me. She would disappear from her bunkmates at times and hide under a bed or behind a tree, which would send her counselors into a panic. I had made it one of my priorities to do a periodic visual check to be sure she had not escaped our supervision.

Before I sat down for dinner or before beginning an evening activity like a campfire, I wanted Cara close by her counselors.

Cara stayed for three weeks during her first

summer at camp. Eve seemed thrilled at her daughter's independence and ability to adjust to a new environment. At the end of the summer season, when I had time to sort out boxes of camp photographs, I noticed how often Cara appeared in camp pictures. Somehow, this vulnerable little camper had become the focus of everyone.

The following winter, Cara's camp application was one of the first to arrive at my home. I assumed her mother felt, as I did, that Cara would be able to build on her positive experience from last summer. Unfortunately, this was not to be the case. When Cara arrived at camp the following summer, she showed early signs that she was struggling. Her disappearing act was happening more frequently, and a few times we found her hiding near the camp parking lot.

After a few days, I decided to call Cara's mother to share my concerns for her daughter's safety. I didn't want to give up on the progress we made the past summer. We all would have felt heartbroken if she had to leave camp early. When we spoke, I suggested that Eve might consider returning to camp to stay over with my wife and me for a few days, in the hope of helping Cara adjust to camp.

I lived at camp in a very rundown cabin by the lake. I had always felt that I should live in the same Spartan style as the rest of the camp. We had an extra room for visitors, but I was embarrassed to offer it to anyone. Our bathroom shower was secured to the wall with duct tape—in true Maine fashion.

It took no persuading on my part; Eve arrived at

camp by noon the following day. Both Cara and her mother seemed delighted to be reunited. That evening after Cara was able to settle down for sleep in her cabin with her bunkmates, Eve sat with us on our porch listening to the loons calling out to each other on the lake.

Eve then shared an extraordinary story of how Cara entered her life. Eve mentioned that she was a published poet. While working on a poem in the quiet hours of the early morning, Eve said she heard a voice deep inside her that told her it was time to give up writing for a while. She felt this intuitive voice wanted her to explore the requirements needed to become a foster parent.

Eve had previously never thought about becoming a foster care provider; however, as a poet, she was accustomed to listening to promptings from her intuition. Eve said that when she shared her new interest with her husband, his first reaction was mostly negative. They already had three children living at home who needed their attention. Their large family was functioning quite well. Why rock the boat?

Their eleven-year-old daughter, named Emma, had extraordinary talent in ballet and had just been hired by the Boston Ballet to perform the lead role of Clara in the Wang Center's performance of the *Nutcracker*. This commitment required long hours of practice. Eve needed to be available to take her daughter to and from rehearsals almost daily until the show concluded on New Year's Day.

Eve assured her husband that he was right; managing their large family was enough of a challenge.

She told him not to worry, she could hardly imagine ever becoming a foster parent. Even after completing all the requirements, Eve was still convinced that nothing would ever come of it.

Twice during the next few months, Eve was contacted by the Boston Department of Social Services to see if she would be interested in meeting a newborn child in need of foster care. Each time she would again assure her husband not to worry when she left the house to view the young infant. Eve said she could hardly believe that she was going through the steps of taking on a newborn; that is, until she was called for the third time.

Eve had tears in her eyes as she told me about meeting the third child referred to her for foster care. Eve said that as soon as she laid eyes on Cara, just five days old, she knew as deeply as she knew anything in her life that Cara was her child. The rest is history including the legal adoption of Cara a few years later.

Just before Eve was about to say goodbye to Cara, she asked if I would be interested in having Cara's older sister, Emma, come up to camp to give a ballet demonstration for the camp. Cara was extremely proud of her sister, and this might give her something to look forward to. I loved the idea. Cara could introduce Emma to everyone and help out with the music for the performance.

This proved to be an extraordinary evening at camp. I knew little about ballet and didn't know what to expect or how the campers might react. Emma was the most graceful dancer I had ever seen. It appeared that she had a different relationship to gravity than we had. She could literally suspend herself in the air as if held up by invisible wires. Our campers loved the performance. Cara beamed with delight and we all gained a deep appreciation for the beauty of ballet.

Sadly, Cara was not able to adjust to camp that summer, even with the two visits from her family. She continued to disappear from her bunkmates and counselors and was once found hiding under one of the camp's vans. I no longer felt that we could provide the supervision Cara needed. Both Eve and I agreed that it was time for Cara to return to the safety of her home and family.

I still think of them often. The story Eve shared that night on my porch is hard to explain; yet I was certain that it was true. We like to think that the events of our lives are scripted in ways that psychologists can decipher. Only rarely do we feel that certain events are just destined to happen and outside of our conscious control. Life finds ways to push us forward into uncharted territory. In Eve's case, it directed her to a life of deep commitment, unconditional love, and spiritual wisdom.

I recently followed up with Cara's family to happily learn that Cara had graduated from college with honors. While supporting herself by managing the paint department of an Ace Hardware store, Cara plans to apply to graduate school to pursue a career in social services.

Father Ken

I remember the day well when Ken first left a message on my office answering machine. I was about to move up to Camp Hawthorne for a new summer season. Staff training began in just two days. My camp van was packed with office equipment, computers, camp files, and personal possessions for a three-month stay on Panther Pond in Raymond, Maine. The last item to be disassembled and packed was my phone answering machine.

When I was about to reach under my desk to unplug the machine, I noticed the red blinking light announcing a new phone message. Parents of campers as well as camp vendors were all aware not to call me at my winter address so close to the opening of camp. I had little patience for telemarketers and honestly felt irritated that I needed to check this one last message before packing the answering machine.

As expected, the message lasted the full four minutes of my tape. It was from a man who was looking for a job running wilderness trips at summer camp. He explained he had just finished a seven-month backpacking trek on the Appalachian Trail and was temporarily living with his parents in Framingham, Massachusetts. He knew it was late to apply for a summer job at camp, but felt that his backpacking adventure could be inspiring to young campers. He stated that he had just taken a year off from teaching elementary school and had experience as a camp counselor.

His voice was gentle and self-assured with a singsong cadence that was pleasant to listen to. It was rare that a counselor applying for a job at our camp would share a desire to inspire young children. Unfortunately, all my staff positions had been filled. I had already run over budget for staff salaries and questioned how an older staff person might gel with younger staff.

At that moment, my Yankee frugality overruled my intuition. With no time to waste, I deleted the message, unplugged the answering machine and headed up to camp. However, I must admit that his voice message lingered in my mind and I questioned whether I had made a hasty decision. I assumed I would forget the whole matter once I arrived at camp.

The following morning I found myself thinking about the man's phone message. I had only a faint memory of his name, but did remember the town he called from since I had once been a special education teacher there. I made a call to directory assistance and within a minute had a phone number that might connect me to this unforgettable voice. I waited a few hours before making the call, just to assure myself that something positive might come out of a conversation with this mystery man.

When the person said, "Hello," I knew I had my man. I explained the process I went through to get his number and that I was slightly haunted by his voice. He said, "I am happy you called; God moves people in wondrous ways." A comment like that might have been a red flag that this man may be way too religious for our staff of many agnostics and religious nonbelievers, however, it was a sentiment I shared, so we agreed to meet each other the following day.

Ken presented himself exactly as I expected. He was bearded with thinning hair, stood five feet ten or so and was thin to the bone from his seven months on the trail. He greeted me like one might greet an old friend from high school. I immediately liked him and was willing to find a place for him. However, my staff was set for our advanced wilderness trips that season. These were coveted positions earned by staff that moved up through the ranks in both responsibility and experience.

We agreed that Ken would head our moderate-level trips geared to younger campers. He would also work closely with me and help out with driving vans and organizing one-and-two-day canoeing and hiking trips. Frankly, I felt Ken would be a good friend and someone

I could trust to tell me how my staff were behaving and performing their responsibilities.

Ken mixed better than I expected with our mostly college-age counselors. He became an instant celebrity once word spread he had just completed backpacking the full 2,189 miles of the Appalachian Trail from Mount Katahdin, Maine, to the summit of Springer Mountain in Georgia.

Ken had one habit that I felt I needed to talk to him about before our campers arrived. Ken found it impossible to refrain from interjecting the phrase "God Bless You" into almost every conversation. I became concerned our camp community might find him odd and not want to associate with him. I needn't have worried. We all soon realized that Ken's religious zeal was authentic. He was truly a warm and loving man who just happened to be overflowing with appreciation and thankfulness for what he believed was God's magnificent creation.

Still I felt it was best for Ken to curb this habit of his. We agreed that he was allowed to say, "God bless you" only three times a day, not including our Sunday chapel service. I knew this was an impossible task for Ken to achieve, but I still felt he needed to put a damper on his verbal religious enthusiasm. This soon became a camp joke and whenever Ken said, "God bless you," a camper or staff would yell out the number one, two or three pertaining to his three allowable blessings. Ken would break into an infectious smile, and we would all have a good laugh at no one's expense. In reality, Ken could not help himself from running way over his three allowable blessings.

During our camp's four-day break between sessions one and two, my wife and I and a few selected staff would drive three vans full of campers to northern Maine for a day of whitewater rafting and then on to Quebec City, Canada, to enjoy the sights and sounds of this historical Canadian city. The day of rafting gave me a few well-earned hours off while the campers and staff rafted the turbulent waters of the Kennebec River.

After a day of rafting and enjoying a fabulous cookout at the rafting facility, we would make our way to the border of Canada and then off to Quebec City. While Quebec City was an opportunity for campers to enjoy what felt like a European City with many historical landmarks, it also posed a significant challenge for me to keep everyone safe and well behaved. Restaurants were extremely lax at checking IDs and were capable of serving a three-olive martini to a fourteen-year-old boy with a milk mustache.

Having Ken along on the trip to help keep our multitude of sinners under control was a must. He was up for the challenge and eager to help me in any way possible.

On the day of our departure to the rafting facility I was feeling extremely anxious. We were under the gun to leave camp by 1:30 in the afternoon in order to arrive at the rafting facility early enough to make dinner and set-up our tents before dark. It was my job to get the three

vans packed with campers, tents, food and passports. If I
was able to gas up our vans and head for the highway by
1:45, I could relax and feel assured we were on schedule.

We arrived at our local Mobil Gas station right on
schedule. I directed each van to park by available gas
pumps. I often thought of myself as part of a NASCAR
pit crew and could shave seconds off our arrival time by
yelling out orders and flying around the gas pumps with
my credit card.

When I got everyone back into the vans, I checked
my mirrors and was ready to exit on to the highway when
I noticed that Ken had gotten out of his van and was
slowly walking over to my van window. I rolled down
the window halfway and immediately knew something
was quite wrong.

Ken appeared with a slight smile on his face. "Ron,"
he said, "we have a problem." "What are you talking
about," was my immediate response. Ken held up a
broken van key and said patiently, "I put the wrong key
in the ignition and when I tried to turn on the engine,
I broke the key inside the ignition."

I rolled down my window until it was fully open so
I could more easily grab Ken by the head and throttle it
against the side of the van's door. Ken held his ground,
"Don't worry Ron, God will provide for us."

Now, I am religious to a point, but not when it
comes to fixing the mechanical problems of my personal
cars and camp vans. I really wanted to wring Ken's neck.
Our reactions to the broken key could not have been

more different. All I could imagine was a four-hour or longer wait to find someone to help us. I assumed we would need the help of a car dealership, but, it was Saturday and all service departments would be closed.

Ken just kept smiling and again repeated his mantra, "God will provide." I was in disbelief and just stared at him. At that moment, as if it came from out of his head, I noticed a white van drive into the gas station with a green sign that read "Acme Locksmith Services."

Was I hallucinating? No, it was true. The nice man in the white van immediately agreed to help us and with the aid of a few tools that he kept in his shirt pocket, was able to dislodge the broken key. Since I try to be prepared for all emergencies, I luckily had an additional set of keys for each van. Within a matter of a few minutes, and twenty dollars for his services, we were again on our way.

I remained mystified for the entire five-hour drive to the campground of the rafting facility. Maybe Ken was on to something.

My Most Perfect Day

❧

Have you ever looked back on your life and wondered why you remember certain events in great detail and others with a faint uncertainty of what really ever happened? Certain memories that go back to my childhood are as clear and well defined to me as anything happening today.

One event from my past stands out as if a shining light from the celestial world lit up my surroundings with a brilliant palate of colors and sounds that I can feel to this day. My story begins during the winter of 2006.

A young woman called my home to ask about renting Camp Hawthorne for her wedding. As the owner of Camp Hawthorne, I received a few scattered calls during the off-season, asking if our camp setting could be rented out for a weekend wedding celebration. Since most couples were interested in the summer months for their wedding, when our children's camp was in full session, I always declined the inquiry. Besides, Camp Hawthorne was built in 1919 and had changed little since its inception. The cabins were built by a local farmer and had no more integrity than a chicken coop. The beds were worn-out army cots. However, the camp setting was breathtaking, with over two miles of pristine shorefront and beaches on Panther Pond.

The caller seemed to have done her research. Both she and her fiancé had already scanned all the pictures and movies on our camp website. They wanted a fall wedding when the leaves were turning. No one was asking for gourmet food. "We are looking for plain camp fare", she said. A standard camp cookout would be fine with a pancake breakfast and a campfire to roast marshmallows with their friends. I tried to dissuade them with images of her walking down to the beach in her wedding gown while tripping over tree roots and chipmunk holes in her four-inch stilettos. She just laughed and asked if it was possible to see the camp that weekend.

It was just after Christmas and I told them the camp road was covered in drifted snow. They said they would rent snowshoes if needed. They were just so excited to see the camp. I met them at the camp gate the following Saturday morning to begin the one-mile trek to the camp setting. They were an adorable couple in their late thirties. I soon learned that they were both cellists with the Boston Symphony Orchestra. Now I understood her desire for a fall wedding, since they performed at Tanglewood, the summer home of the renowned orchestra.

We hiked around the camp and peeked into a few of the boarded-up buildings. They acted like little children, giggling in unison and taking in every detail of the camp with fresh eyes. I was having a really nice time sharing camp stories with them. They were impressed when I told them my younger son and I were both taking cello lessons and that we had a recital the next day. The other performers were all under eleven years old except for me. When we returned to their car at the end of our visit, they insisted on giving me a deposit to secure the date for their wedding. There was no way I could disappoint them. The wedding was on.

They told me to expect sixty-five or so guests. This was to be a wedding party for their many friends in the orchestra. They assured me they would all appreciate the rustic atmosphere and authenticity of my camp. It was the off-season, so I had trouble hiring anyone to help me with cooking and cleanup. I was able to secure the help of one of my counselors named Alex, who was still living at the camp, as he planned his next career move. I am not a professional cook, but somehow felt I could pull off the weekend celebration.

The weather was perfect as the wedding party gathered on our beach for a 6:00 pm ceremony. I had the area set up with camp benches facing the lake. Some of our red maple trees by the lake were blazing red as the sun slowly dipped toward the lake. I had brought down a picnic table for champagne and glasses so guests could toast the new couple. I wanted to make their wedding as special as I could so I surprised them by serving a large tray of cheeses, smoked meats, shrimp, and fruit and carried it down to the beach with considerable fanfare. For a slight moment, I felt like the chef of a swanky Manhattan Italian restaurant.

The cookout went as planned. Everyone gathered around my pinewood fire to watch me flip paper-thin hamburgers and roll hotdogs on a cast iron grill. Once dinner cleanup was over, I set up a campfire for them by the beach. On my way up the hill toward my cabin, I noticed a corral of classical instruments in expensive travel cases by the door of our lodge building. A wedding guest shared that they all wanted the full camp experience. After the beach campfire and traditional marshmallow roast, they planned to move into the lodge for a camp-style talent show.

The following morning was sunny but cold for October in Maine. I plugged in the sixty-cup coffee percolator around six, expecting my guests to arrive in the kitchen at daybreak. It would be difficult to sleep late on such a cold morning. The only heat in the kitchen came from the surface of the gas grill that needed a full half hour to be brought up to temperature to handle the 300 or so pancakes I estimated I would need for this group.

I was more than capable of putting on a show for our guests. With spatulas in each hand, I flipped the pancakes with lightning speed while carrying on a conversation with many of my guests. Some of the guests shared that they always wanted to try out their hand as a short-order cook. "Well, here's your chance," I said as I handed over my utensils. Six or so men gave it a try while the others sipped their coffee. My guests may have been the greatest musicians in the country, but they were clueless working a camp pancake grill.

I felt sad saying goodbye to my friendly guests. They were scheduled to leave by 11:00, but many wanted to spend the full day on the beach, which was fine with me. A more gracious group you could not find anywhere. I was tired after cleanup and wanted to head home. On my departure out of camp, I stopped by the lodge to make sure all the lights were turned off. When I opened the door, I was amazed to see four cello players sitting by a large pile of printed music. They asked if it would be all right for them to use the lodge to play some music together that one of the cellists wanted to share with the group.

I was a bit startled by their request. "Of course," I said, "I love cello music." Then the cellist sharing the music said I should stay and they would play a cello concert just for me. "Oh my God, that is wonderful," I said, " just give me a minute to get a comfortable chair." I ran to my house to retrieve a soft canvas chair I bought at LL Bean.

I set up my chair just fifteen feet in front of the four musicians. The camp lodge had a hip-roof design with a low ceiling. The floor and walls were made of white pine. I knew the acoustics were going to be extraordinary.

They seemed interested to know if I had any particular composer in mind that I wanted them to play. My response was that I enjoyed schmaltzy cello music. "Let's see if you can make me cry," I said. And cry I did. The rustic melodies they played wafted around me from all sides. The building was the perfect music box to experience these four cellists of paramount abilities. While I listened to the music, I looked out the lodge windows at the lake. It was a lovely day in the high sixties with only fair weather clouds and no humidity. The lake was cobalt blue.

For almost two hours I sat in my chair, spellbound by the music and the musicianship of my guests. I couldn't believe my good fortune. When the music stopped I was so filled with emotion I could hardly walk the few feet to my car. This was my most perfect day.

The Guardian Angel

M y life's work as a camp director ended abruptly when I received word that our lease on the camp property was not going to be renewed. This news was completely unexpected. I now faced the awesome task of selling off all the camp equipment and cleaning out the buildings for the new tenant. I was feeling as low as I had ever felt in my life. All the work and improvements that were done around camp over the past twenty-four summers were hard-fought. Every chair and bench I made for the camp in my wood shop over the many winters was full of memories. I raised my children as well as hundreds of other children at the camp, and all were dear to my wife and me. The burden of now having to sell everything off and take tons of old equipment to the dump was more than I could bear.

A friend suggested that I contact other camp directors in Maine, to let them know what was for sale or for the taking. Within minutes of sending out emails, my two phones started ringing off the hook. I must have talked to twenty camp owners in the first hour, all sharing their condolences but also eager to see what I had for sale. I decided to meet with everyone at my camp over the next week. They each agreed to arrive with a truck or trailer to remove whatever they wanted to purchase.

It was on that day that I first talked to Dennis, who was from a small Christian camp near midcoast Maine. Dennis wanted to meet me at my camp the following morning. The prices I was asking didn't seem to matter to him at all. I had fifty bunk beds that cost me over $500 each and were only a few years old. I was asking $140 apiece, which, I felt, was a fair price. Dennis said he was coming with a check and that he wanted all he could get into his truck and trailer. He sounded different from the other camp people I had talked to that morning. He said he looked forward to our meeting the following day.

Dennis called me twice early the next morning to assure me he would arrive on time. He was a slender sixty-five-year-old man and appeared to be in excellent health and very capable of carrying the heavy bed frames up the hill from the children's cabins to his truck. He could see I was in considerable pain, both physically and emotionally, as I struggled to help with the beds. After a few trips, we stopped by the lake under a large pine tree for me to catch my breath. It was then that Dennis gently inquired about what had happened with my camp.

I felt a deep sense of peace and love coming from

this man I had only known for a few minutes. In an attempt to share my story with Dennis, I fell into uncontrollable sobbing. Dennis put his arm around my shoulders and repeated that it would all be okay and that I was a good man. He sat with me for over an hour, absorbing my deep catharsis of emotion. As the day continued, we would move a few more beds up the hill for twenty minutes or so and then sit on the ground to talk about our lives, as honestly and deeply as I had ever talked to anyone before.

I assumed Dennis was a camp owner or director or at least a camp caretaker. He said he was only a volunteer trying to help out the camp. He began to share a little about his life. Dennis grew up dirt poor in the backwoods of Maine with two unemployed parents and four sisters. He said the house had little heat and no insulation. Each morning it was his job to carry water from an outside hand pump and heat it over the wood stove so that his sisters could each take turns with the same bath water to get clean for school. Dennis stated he had little interest in being the fifth person to bathe in the same bath water. All he could remember eating on any day of his youth was potatoes with mustard. Growing up, he never even saw money and felt his parents had no income and lived on what they could grow in their garden and help from their church and town charities.

After high school, Dennis enlisted in the Air Force and was amazed that he would receive a salary of seventeen dollars a week. "What would I ever do with all this money?" he said. Dennis had never had any money and had little use for it. He later married a social worker and adopted two special needs children. Now he was retired from the Air Force and felt compelled to give most of the money away he received each month from his retirement. Dennis said, "Why would I need money when if I need anything, someone is always eager to give it to me?"

We talked more than we worked that day. When all the beds he could transport were loaded onto his truck and trailer, we added up the total to be over $3,000. I had also given him free mattresses for all the beds. Dennis handed me a check. When I examined it, I saw it was a personal check. I asked him why the check was not from the camp he was buying them for. He laughed and said he was buying them with his own money for the camp because they needed them. "Dennis," I explained, "I can't let you do this. I have money saved for myself and family, you have nothing, so how can I let you pay for them?"

His deep and natural sense of giving was uprooting all my ideas of saving money for security, emotional safety, and status. I told him he was ruining my life with his example of giving away all that he had. I fought with him for most of an hour to just take the beds as a gift from me, but he would have none of it. In our financial stalemate, he finally agreed that he would purchase them at half the price I was asking, so that I could feel I was contributing too. Dennis just looked at me and smiled.

"Ron, you're a good man," he repeated with a wave of his hand as he drove out of camp.

Once his truck had disappeared down the camp road, I called my wife at work and told her that I had just met Clarence, the guardian angel from the Christmas movie *It's a Wonderful Life*. I have never forgotten what Dennis taught me by the example of his life. I did some research and found out that it was true that Dennis would give away most of the money he received from his retirement each month and that everyone in town and at the camp loved to give back to him as well. Dennis truly found a holy balance of how to live gracefully in our material world. I think of him often.

Memories of Campers and Staff

𝕾

Emma Schulman, Camper, 2001-2010

Over eight years have passed since I was a camper at Camp Hawthorne. Still there are so many reminders that bring me back to Panther Pond: the smell of the pine trees, the cry of the loons, the feeling of a campfire warming my face, a funny song, my lack of competitive spirit for anything other than building a parade float, and the happiness I feel when I eat a grilled cheese sandwich and tomato soup for lunch. Six years of looking up to my amazing counselors taught me to strive to be a better person. Friday night camp dances taught me to dance however I want to dance, and not care what other people think. Sunday morning chapel taught me to try to live my life according to the words of our chapel song "Give Yourself to Love." And bunk inspection taught me that anyone can be bribed with candy.

Camp was a magical place filled with magical people. Ron convinced me to come to camp by slightly overstating the magic—telling me that, astoundingly, mosquitoes don't come to Camp Hawthorne. My first day at camp I was scared and lonely. I was leaving my twin sister for the first time. I was sleeping on the top bunk for the first time and quickly noticed the collection of spiders that hung out in the bathroom cabin. The first night, one of my counselors, perhaps noticing my nervousness, grabbed my hands and pulled me into a dance, spinning and twirling me until I forgot my uneasiness. As I danced on the shore of Panther Pond I felt some of my tension melt away, and then even more of it faded at the opening campfire. While I sat with my back against a log and my shoulders touching those of my new friends, I watched as Ron—the most amazing storyteller I will ever meet—tell us a dramatic tale of bravery and peril. I was completely entranced. I didn't even notice the mosquitoes biting my legs.

Julia Levine, Camper, 2003-2011

When I think back about my childhood and all the different experiences that contributed to me being the person I am today, I can only think exclusively of Camp Hawthorne. I thank my father every chance I get for the opportunity he gave me and my brother to attend Hawthorne.

I remember the first time I set foot on the grounds, nestled at the end of David Plummer Rd. We were dropping off my older brother to begin his first summer at camp. I saw the bunk 1 cabin for the youngest girls and read the poem painted on the outside wall written by Dr. Seuss. I immediately begged my dad to let me stay. I felt instantly that this place was special, and I wanted to be part of it. My parents did ask, but it would not be possible that summer. When we arrived home, however, I made him register me for the summer of 2003.

I was so excited to finally arrive, as a tiny pip-squeak of seven-years-old, to experience all the incredible things my brother had told me about throughout the year. Now I could make my own stories to tell. The general feeling I get when I think back about camp is still so powerful, that I seem to carry it with me every day. I would dream of someday being a counselor at Hawthorne, after I made it through all five girls' cabins. I even loved doing KP in the kitchen at camp, blasting music while we would sweep the dining room and kitchen after we scrubbed all the dishes.

I can still remember how it feels to rig up the green FJ sailboat and push off from shore to sail my way around Panther Pond. It was just nonstop fun at camp, no matter how cliché it may sound. I know camp shaped me: from weekly chapel where I would repeatedly say how thankful I was to get the opportunity to yet again return to camp.

Sweat lodge was always a challenge for me. It required a moment of pride and strength as I would overcome my fears of claustrophobia so I could connect with all my friends and counselors on a deeper level. I can remember being faced with a level of independence that was foreign to me and how I was forced to navigate it myself, because my "too-cool" older brother wanted nothing to do with me at camp.

I still remember what the cabins smelled like. I remember every rock in the ground as I would walk outside the lodge at night to fill up my water bottle. I loved the sounds of the loons and of the water lapping on the shore each morning when I woke up. Writing my memories has become a stream of consciousness. I feel an overpowering sense of happiness and sadness overcome me. I will never forget the day I found out our camp was gone. I cried endlessly and could not fathom what my life would be like without it. Would I never have another Fenway Day where Ron hit a grand slam? Never another Casco Day Parade? Never another Color Wars swim meet or our Civil War game trying to capture General Robin Clark.

I think of my happiest memories, moments of greatest challenges and accomplishments, and the best friends I've ever made being a product of camp. Camp Hawthorne is me, and I am camp.

Wendy Traynor, Parent of three campers: Hannah, Dana, and Baird, 2003-2010

"You always go stag to the Hawthorne dances."

As a child I went to camp for eight summers so I get camp. I loved camp. However, Camp Hawthorne was not like other overnight camps. It was a fantasy dream that my kids got to actually live every summer for eight years. At camp, your age, gender, or background did not matter. What did matter was kindness, respect, fun, laughter, soulfulness, Robinson Crusoe tree houses, archery, zombie apocalyptic games, good deeds, manhunt games, the beach and Ron's Sunday morning homemade donuts. . . . those were important.

We became a camp family 365 days a year. Not a day went by when I did not hear a camp story or a camp reference or see a camp tee shirt on one of my children. We all counted down the days until camp would begin. My three children could not wait to get back to their people and their place and their soulful and unconventional leader.

My children were enchanted by Camp Hawthorne. The first year I drove down Plummer Road to drop off my children, I arrived at a clearing with a tetherball post and picnic tables. I saw big kids walking with little kids and talking and hanging out together. Parents even looked like they were there for the summer too. Musical instruments came out of cars. Music was in the air and everyone was hugging. Ron and Diane were everywhere warmly welcoming everyone and joyously catching up. That first summer, I got into my car hesitant to leave my kids. The second summer I just did not want to leave the camp and the scene.

Ron and Diane and their amazing counselors created an escape from the real world into another real world. One summer I came up for a visit and was able to stay for dinner. Bunks sat and laughed together and then came the announcements. That evening there was a power point presentation of the day's fishing derby. The counselor put together a newsy and very home made presentation about fishing tackle, possible catches, and weather conditions with constant commentary from the campers and in the end we found out that no one had caught a fish. The video was hilariously pointless and yet it captured the essence of Hawthorne. The point of everything is to be willing and to take the journey.

We were hooked on the Hawthorne vibe. At the end of the camp season, I told Ron that we needed a nanny to help out at my home while I was at work each day. I said we just had to have someone from Hawthorne. We were able to hire Julie for two years and then Ron's son Asa for another two. When they stayed for dinner, our family would talk about something that happened during the day that somehow related to something at camp.

One night, my oldest daughter had a dozen camp friends over for a sleepover in the middle of the winter. We roasted marshmallows and made smores. One of the campers started telling the beginning of one of Ron's campfire stories imitating Ron's distinct New England accent. Spontaneously, the kids went around the table picking up on Ron's story where the other had left off, all in Ron's voice, until the entire story was told. In the moment they were all profoundly connected and there was tears and laughter.

On Columbus Day, following the final closing of Camp Hawthorne, my children and I drove up to camp to say goodbye to the place that had been their solace and serenity for years. We were all sitting on the beach with a counselor who had come up to help Ron close up the camp for the last time. At one point the counselor rolled up his pants and waded into the water to sing the Hawthorne version of John Denver's song, "Take Me Home Country Road." The sound echoed across the water and then my three children respectfully and tearfully joined in from afar singing "Take me home to the place I belong . . ."

Kelsey Barrett Fink, Camper and Staff, Waterfront Director, 1996-2009

When the time came to go to overnight camp when I was nine years old, I struggled to separate from my parents. Thankfully, they made me stay and I could not be more thankful. As a child, I was painfully shy. I hated to be the center of attention. As a camper, I met people who were open and kind. I was able to come out of my shell and make the type of friendships that I never knew existed. I got through some of the most painful years of my life by leaning on these friendships in the summer and staying in touch throughout the school year. So much of who I am is because of Camp Hawthorne, but I am certainly not the only person who would say this.

Camp Hawthorne was so important to me that I found a way to continue going as a teenager and as an adult. I lived every camper's dream and worked in the kitchen, the office, and eventually became a bunk counselor and the waterfront director. I became a mentor to campers and did my best to guide them as well as my counselors guided me. I ran terrified from campers in Manhunt, I sat transfixed during Campfire as others told stories and sang songs, I painted my entire body blue for a skit, I gave countless campers cornrows, I cleaned the bathrooms, I ate toilet paper soaked with chocolate pudding, I taught campers how to solve a Rubik's Cube and got some interested in solving logic puzzles, and I certified campers and counselors as lifeguards. My fellow campers and counselors knew me better than anyone. I yearned for Sunday mornings when I could refresh my body with the egg of light meditation.

Now, as a parent, I sing "Give Yourself To Love" every night to my son. I miss those years, but I am incredibly thankful that I was able to spend seventeen summers at camp. I am thankful for the relationships I made and the knowledge that they will last for my entire life even when I cannot find the time to keep in touch.

Llora Kressman (Holman), Camper, 1986-1995

I said a boom chicka boom, I said a boom-a chicka rocka chicka rocka chicka boom . . . Camp Hawthorne, the songs, the chants, the loons, the art. Ron and Diane, Asa and Peter. Panther Pond. The crazy counselors, the dances, the bug juice, the rope swing, Chapel, sailing, swimming in Panther Pond. Campfires. That immense, endless starry sky over the Field. Sweat lodges. Friends coming back year after year, Hawthorne was my favorite place on earth from the time I was eight until I turned sixteen. It probably still is, even though the camp is closed and I have never been back. Camp Hawthorne saved my little life. At eight, I was a tiny, sensitive, tow-headed, shy little girl. My parents had just divorced, ending a chaotic chapter filled with anger and alcoholism. I was a mess. We knew Ron and Diane from the Unitarian Universalist Church in Portsmouth, New Hampshire. That's how my mother found Camp Hawthorne.

I spent half the summer and eventually all summer at Camp Hawthorne. Each summer two sessions of Sailing Camp followed by two sessions of Arts Camp. I attended Sailing Camp for umpteen years but couldn't sail one of those Flying J's to save my life (well maybe I could). But this is exactly, believe it or not, what made camp what it was for me. Sailing was good, but I didn't come to learn to sail. And that was just fine. I loved everything else about camp and wanted to be there as long as I possibly could. Being barefoot all day, sleeping in those rickety, ancient cabins, only a thin bug-holed screen between me and the outdoors, the sense of freedom and so much silliness. I loved how I felt at camp.

I did learn to sail, canoe, batik, watercolor, tie dye, many things. But really I was learning how to be a little girl. I remember once sitting at the top of the hill outside the Rec Hall when a friend passed by and asked if I was going to the dance that night. I said I didn't know. I thought I probably danced too weird. My nine-year-old friend told me, at Camp Hawthorne "the weirder you dance, the better." That's what made camp so special. That is pretty much why camp was what it was for me. That freedom to be exactly who I was. The wildness, weirdness and sense of freedom, belonging and acceptance transformed me.

All of it, of course, being held by the ever-watchful, Ron (and his bull horn). The freedom and wildness were only beneficial because I knew Ron was watching and that he was a hardass. We could only go so far. I was afraid of him, but I also knew that he loved me. I don't know how he did it with so many campers coming and going all summer long, but I always had the sense that Ron knew me, who I really was, that he got me. The sense of being seen made me feel utterly and totally safe all of the time. So I took safe risks, and, gradually, came out of my protective shell.

Each summer I couldn't wait to come back. And, my mother sent me back, year after year, because when she picked me up from camp, coming down that long, dirt driveway, bumping over all of those roots and rocks, I was transformed. I was happy, confident, and talkative. I was beaming. I was myself. Camp Hawthorne saved my little life, and, in so many ways, it has shaped my life. It's one of the best things that has ever happened to me.

Denise Anderson, Theatre Director, 2009

One wintery day, Ron, his wife Diane, and the spritely Cullen came to Pennsylvania to meet me, and they changed the direction of my life. Swooping me up into their funnel of magic and charisma, I was entranced and engaged, so there was really only one choice for this girl who had never been to sleep away camp, but whose lost soul somehow needed to be found and nourished by the wisdom of Maine's enchanted landscape and the bohemian tribe residing therein—I was hired, and off I went!

Aside from the mystical and mirthful experience directing and watching campers perform in the woods by Panther Pond, my summer spent as Camp Hawthorne gave me a place to call home in my heart forevermore. Within Camp Hawthorne's serene grounds, myself and many others were able to quiet our restless souls. Now, as I walk through life, in times of joy, in times of sorrow, in times of confusion or frustration, in times of trouble, in times of euphoric happiness, the peace of Camp Hawthorne can bring me back to grounded stillness, and it calls me to trust in it, believe in its ability to heal and awaken and guide my soul. I cherish it. Thank you, Ron for this intangible gift of faith.

Deena Bahu, Staff, 2000-2009

What does camp mean to me? The exact same thing it meant to me on July 12, 2006 when I wrote about camp from the top of Quaker Ridge at sunset:

> *I am now 100% convinced that living richly, living in the moment, and making happiness and adventure a priority—are what's really important in life. I have been trying to live that way.*

Camp Hawthorne wasn't just a place I went to in the summer. It was a place I gave up everything to go back to as a counselor every summer after I graduated from college (when I should have been focused on "building my professional network and career in New York City"). Why? Because Ron's experiment in "the art of living" was more than an experiment. It was a lesson in being.

When thinking of what camp means to me, I am also reminded of something I wrote at camp while teaching creative writing at the Chapel one afternoon. I asked the Bunk 6 campers to pull out a writing prompt from my famous Michigan State University hat and write for ten minutes about whatever came to mind.

I always participated. I selected prompt #34: What was the most interesting place that I have ever visited? I wrote about Camp Hawthorne.

> *It's a place where*
> *laughter rules*

and tears are smothered with hugs.
Where pounding
on the furniture during meal time
is promoted
and it is
ALWAYS
okay to be dirty.

Brett Stithem, Staff, 2000-2003

I owe a great debt to Camp Hawthorne. My first summer was almost twenty years ago and the friendships I formed back then continue to grow. The camp, which was selected seemingly at random in what was probably one of my first ever internet searches, would become one of the pivotal experiences of my life. I knew within a few days of my arrival, that Camp Hawthorne, under Ron Furst's intentional direction, was a place where one's defenses to forming close and caring relationships, seemed silly and unnecessary.

Camp Hawthorne was a vision created by Ron, soon shared by all the staff and then passed on to the campers. The result was a heady marriage of living with deep purpose and spontaneity. I know I am just one of many former counselors and campers who have spent the rest of our lives drawing from these experiences of community, friendship, and joy, and then finding some way to share them with the world.

Jessica Tkacik, Camper and Staff, 1996-2010

Camp Hawthorne meant the world to me. I grew up there, physically and emotionally. It was my coming of age where I learned what kind of person I wanted to be and slowly became it. As a camper and a counselor, the unique and refreshing thing was that the campers were truly treated as young adults. We were trusted. It was expected that at our core everyone knows right from wrong and you were expected to make the right choice. There was no need for a list of overbearing rules. If we made mistakes, there were always people willing to support and guide you. Many of the most important people in my life have come directly from Camp Hawthorne. I think for the rest of my life that what I have learned at camp will be my guiding compass.

Josh Eilberg, Camper and Film Staff, 1987-2009

My only experience with overnight camp, prior to Camp Hawthorne, was a soccer camp when I was seven years old. Being the youngest camper and not a competitive person by nature, it turned out to be a miserable experience for me. I was understandably resistant to the idea of another overnight camp experience. The following year my dad and I were able to meet with Ron who somehow convinced us both to give Camp Hawthorne a try. Almost immediately, I noticed that this camp was different. Ron really created a family atmosphere in a non-competitive environment and everyone was encouraged to be themselves.

Over the next twenty-four years, Camp Hawthorne became a second home to me. Looking back over my time there with all my memories, two events stand out that sum up what it means to be a part of the Camp Hawthorne family. On August 19th, 1991, Hurricane Bob devastated the New England region and left camp without power for more than a week. Ron assured worried parents that their children would be safe and camp would go on. After spending a night in a gymnasium at a nearby school, camp resumed without power and everyone really came together to create new experiences and memories.

The other memory that comes to mind was in the summer of 2000. Just before camp started, I lost my brother in a car accident. As I struggled to deal with this tragedy, camp became a safe place to get away from the sadness back home. Having a supportive camp family really allowed me the opportunity to get through this difficult time.

As the actual camp experience slips further into the past, the memories are as fresh as though they happened yesterday. The other thing that has endured are the friendships that came from camp. They are more than friendships . . . they are family.

Kelsey Le Gloahec, Staff, 2007-2010

When I heard our chapel song "Give Yourself to Love" for the first time, I was moved in such a way as when the wind moves the tall pines of the forest beside the beloved Panther Pond. Sunday morning, our chapel time, was this ever-connected time that shone with light and love when we sang our song, holding each other arm in arm. I had been going to church all my life and yet it was in that chapel moment that I felt truly home and fully connected. I could be—not just do, feel—not just watch. I still tear up when I hear that song.

Danny Parker, Staff, 2000-2004

I came to Camp Hawthorne for the first time in the summer of 2000. I was twenty-five years old and had been working in Manhattan as a news editor. On the side I played in a struggling rock 'n' roll band. Neither the excitement of midtown Manhattan nor the lights of Soho were as rewarding as I'd expected, and I had become disillusioned. I drank too much and grew gloomier with each passing year.

Hired by Ron as a camp counselor, little did I know when I arrived at the top of the hill on David Plummer Road and caught my first glimpse of Panther Pond that my life was about to change forever. At Camp Hawthorne children and adults learned to love and trust one another and friendships formed lasted a lifetime. It was a place where positivity and respect for people and nature reigned and where the thick layers of social strata and prejudice peeled away.

The camp and its people reawakened my senses, and parts of my persona from childhood reemerged. The smell of the campfire, the glow of the moon on the water, the soft browns of the forest floor—a thousand joys began to surface in me, and I reconnected to nature like a lost lover.

When I arrived, Ron was already in his eighteenth year as owner and director of Camp Hawthorne. His charismatic and thoughtful nature was the guiding force of all who worked and played there. He could be a wacky, wise-guy comedian entertaining the kids in the dining hall with his infectious silliness, and moments later calmly instill a profound teaching into the conscience of the group.

Behind the scenes he worked his ass off, barely sleeping for the two months the community was his responsibility. He took his duties seriously, walking the grounds with a flashlight while we snored in our bunks. In the off-season he would trudge through snow drifts to clear the roofs of the cabins and make sure the old bunks were protected.

Diane was an equal wonder at camp. Brilliantly zany and full of wit, drawn to the youngest children and the awkward teens, she was both hilarious and serious, caring, and always refreshingly honest. The front porch of their house served as an open-air counseling parlor where the discourse could veer in a hundred directions. It was one of the few places at camp where adults could get away from the campers for a while, and Diane and Ron always provided wise counsel.

Over the course of the summer, the community knit itself together, and I'd begun to confide in new friends of all ages about my uncertain status once summer was over. I realized I couldn't go back to New York. "What should I do? Buy a cheap car and travel?" A common response from my fellow counselors, who lived and attended school across the country, was "Come visit me!"

By the time August arrived, my heart overflowed with love and appreciation—for Ron and Diane, the other counselors, the staff, and, of course, the campers. Days full of moments: Waking in the bunk with a bunch of sleepy, mumbling boys who were like a herd of little brothers; waiting in line for breakfast with campers, discussing important issues like Capture the Flag strategies; Fluffer Nutter preparation techniques; kayaking plans, music, Shakespeare, or fart jokes; writing songs or poetry with campers while sitting on logs in the forest; walks in the woods; milk-and-cookie times; epic Ultimate Frisbee matches; paddling out to the island or across the lake to the inlet with the rope swing; nights on duty telling stories or strumming my guitar so kids would fall asleep, or off duty raiding the cereal bar with other counselors.

I stuck around for a few weeks after camp was over helping Ron board up the cabins and polishing off the leftover food from the freezers. As September blew in and the evenings grew cooler, Ron took me around to some used car dealers in Windham and Lewiston and taught me the art of the haggle. He found me a great deal on a Chevy, and with that purchase my plan solidified: the next ten months took me through forty-four states to some incredible adventures on the West Coast, and to a surprising new career as a traveling environmental activist. I headed back to Maine the following June for another magical summer.

Camp Hawthorne gave me five unforgettable summers, lifelong friends, and countless cherished memories. My experience as a counselor added points to my resume and gave me a foot in the door to a teaching career now in its fifteenth year.

Much love to all in our Camp Hawthorne community and hey, if you're ever in Portland, Oregon, come visit me!

Cam Jones, Camper, 2003-2009

In February of 2003, my father had just passed away. I was restless and grieving and needed to go somewhere— anywhere. My mom asked me to go with her to a local camp fair in Portland, Maine, in search of a camp. That is where I met Ron. I was quickly sold on attending the film program at Camp Hawthorne the coming summer.

From that day on, I felt that we had found a place

I could belong. The Hawthorne philosophy helped me through some of the darkest times in my life and still continues to do so. I owe a lot to what camp has brought me in my life. I just would not be the person that I am today. I would not know all the incredible people I know today and would not have the same outlook on life. Not a day goes by that I have not thought about all those incredible summers. Every life touched by Camp Hawthorne is blessed with more than just great memories. They have been given the tools to live a rich life.

Haley Peltz, 1998-2007

I started hearing music at camp. I had heard it before on the radio, but it made more sense when I saw campers and counselors singing in a circle around our campfire and when others sang along. I became interested in songs that made people put their arms around one another and the ones that made them cry. What was so special about those songs.

The musical venues at camp allowed for a privileged kind of listening. The campfires, chapel, the coffee houses—they were quiet, listening times, different from the rest of camp. There was a holiness in the space that allowed for the performance of a song. It was like the people who came forward to sing were sharing a beautiful **secret**. Many of the songs performed in these spaces took on levels of meaning to me. They came to signify friendship, family, and love itself.

There were times where I heard myself sing, and others heard me. My current ideas about performing and creating an experience where people want to listen and perhaps sing along, come largely from my musical experiences at Camp Hawthorne. How precious to be able to think my way back to those times.

www.ingramcontent.com/pod-product-compliance
Lightning Source LLC
Chambersburg PA
CBHW052112090426
42741CB00009B/1775